THE ~~LITTLE~~ *my*my

BOOK OF

MOTIVATION

MAGIC

The tools, strategies and methods to show you just what's possible, if you know where to look and what to do

LARA DOHERTY

The ~~Little~~ Mighty Book of Motivation Magic

ISBN 978-1-907308-32-1
First published in the UK by Compass-Publishing UK, 2021.
Typeset and Edited by The Book Refinery Ltd.
www.thebookrefinery.com

Cover design by Grace Milas Design

The right of Lara Doherty to be identified as the author of this work has been asserted by her in accordance with the Copyright, Designs and Patents Act 1988.

www.themotivationclinic.co.uk

Printed and bound by CMP, Dorset, UK.

This book has been produced using Carbon Capture paper, creating native woodland in the UK.

Lara Doherty is not a medical doctor, dietician, nutritionist, psychologist or neuroscientist, nor does she hold a degree in medicine, dietetics, nutrition, psychology or neuroscience, and she makes no claims to having any specialised medical training. The content within this book is not intended to diagnose or treat any condition, but it is provided for informational, educational, and self-improvement purposes only. Please make your own well-informed decisions based upon what is best for you.

Dedication

*This book is dedicated to anyone who has ever got to a
stage in their life and thinks,* Is this it?

*My parents, my family, my friends, my clients and everybody I mention
in the following pages – all of you made this book possible. Thank you. xo*

WHAT PEOPLE ARE SAYING...

I was lucky enough to work with Lara in a recent period of my life where I needed support, direction and motivation. She was a lifeline and a ray of sunshine. Her knowledge of coaching and the psychology behind our actions was so helpful in moving me forward from a place of overwhelm, and I looked forward to our weekly meetups for the energy they would give me and the level of understanding that she offered. I would highly recommend Lara to anyone who has a vision but needs accountability and motivation to move forward with their plans.

~ Sarah M

I first met Lara [when I was] feeling overwhelmed and confused on where I was and where I was going. Through compassion and different techniques, Lara has managed to help me find clarity, direction and inner peace. I feel motivated, with a clearer path and purpose, and with a new found energy. I really can't recommend Lara enough.

~ Jemima R

I loved working with Lara. I was recommended her vision board workshops as a way of looking at what I wanted for my business, but what I got was so much more. I went on to do some coaching, which helped me gain insight and clarity, mainly personally, but which had a knock-on effect in all aspects of my life. Lara is very good at gently holding you accountable and encouraging you to move and grow with your findings, and of course, the vision board(s) you do with her are there as a visual reminder. I'm in awe of how much of it has come into fruition. A fun, compassionate and professional experience that I am more than happy to recommend to others.

~ Karen D

Lara is THE person who can guide you, with the use of vision boards, to help work out where you want to be and coach you on how to get there. She has a wealth of professional experience behind her, which serves to keep you on track, focused and motivated. She's like your cheerleader rooting for your success, leading the way for investment in your future self-development. I cannot recommend her highly enough.

~Hazel T

"It is never too late to be what you might have been."

— George Eliot

Contents

"Feeling better is temporary. Transformation is forever."

— Christine Kane

INTRODUCTION

Here's my ~~Little~~ [or not so little] *Mighty Book of Motivation Magic*, a book you can carry in your pocket, in your handbag, in your backpack or have by the loo, and turn to a page, learn something new, feel encouraged, and be empowered and motivated to carry on and to never give up...

What the book is about

This book has been four and a half years in the making. In my previous life, it may have been called *From Rock Bottom to Empowerment – A Memoir*; however, as I didn't want to dwell on the past, but wished to focus on the present and, most definitely, on the positive, the new me and an exciting future, this book was born!

I hope you enjoy reading it as much as I've enjoyed writing it. I've always wanted to celebrate all the amazing inspirational people, books, talks, tools and methods that I've discovered over the last few years and used as my motivation and power to rise up from rock bottom.

Perhaps you've lost purpose, like I did, or you've never really been sure what having purpose means or what that feels like exactly? Perhaps you've been meandering through life without a care in the world and turning 40-plus just slapped you in the face like a wet fish? Maybe you've lost your mojo and feel rudderless or lost at sea, flailing around with no sense of direction and no idea how to move forwards?

What I'd say is this: if you have even the tiniest inkling inside you that you want to change your life, but might be too scared to, or you don't have a clue how to move forwards and change, then this book will be your support, your guide and encouragement, and the voice in your head saying that you can totally do this (with bells on!) and imagine your life if you don't.

I've learnt that taking baby steps towards a better future is the way to go; surround yourself with the dreamers and the doers, the believers and the thinkers, but most of all, surround yourself with those who see greatness within you – even when you don't see it yourself!

How to read this book

Start here.

This book has been written using the exact same process through which my transformation took place. It all started with making a *decision*: I no longer wanted to feel miserable, unhappy, and lacking in direction and confidence; to be unable to fit comfortably into any of my clothes, and feel bloated and unattractive; and to hate what I saw in the mirror. I wanted to have a purposeful life that's full of fun and adventure, look great, feel great, and be happy – and I was determined to work out how to do that!

As you read through the book, it would be great to have a notebook handy, as there will be a few exercises to complete as you go along, and a notebook is also a really useful place in which to write and record any thoughts and feelings you have as you go through this process.

Setting an intention to change

Everything starts with intention. Think of it as the start of a journey: you're in your car, and you type the postcode into your satnav or phone, which will eventually take you to your destination, with a few traffic jams and roadworks on the way. Sometimes, just making that decision to leave the house can be the biggest hurdle to overcome, particularly when you feel stuck and at a crossroads, and you don't know which path to take next.

It may feel like you're trapped on a hamster wheel or floundering at sea; at the time, I remember I called it "wading through treacle" and "feeling flattened like a very ripe peach on a pavement". Excitingly, intention has the power to truly change your life and push you towards a destination, with or without a global pandemic!

As humans, we get mired and stuck in our familiar patterns; the familiar is safer than doing something new and different. Small, consistent baby steps of change and remembering what you're leaving behind will make it easier.

If the change you want is to feel motivated, positive, driven, creative, resilient, innovative, hopeful and confident, and you wish to gain clarity, excitement and focus in different areas of your life, then this book will help you throughout that process. All of the tools, methods and strategies in the pages of this book are tried and tested, and my transformation is a true testament to them working; I discovered them through hours of online research and drowning in personal-development material – as much of it as I could take in!

If I can do it, you can do it too. Yes, you do have to dig deep and work hard at it, but honestly, the rewards are endless and keep on giving, like ripples across the ocean. You'll discover things about yourself and others in your life, about your mind and thoughts, and most importantly, about who you really are and all of the amazing gifts you have to give to the world. Now take my hand, and off we go.

"It always seems impossible until it's done."

– Nelson Mandela

A word of cautionary advice

This book has been written during the global COVID-19 pandemic. As we seem to be coming out the other side of this (at the time of writing), I think it's important to reflect on how this may have affected our mental health. My mental health has certainly taken a bashing during this time, like that of so many others, and although this book is meant to be a positive, uplifting and motivational book, it would be remiss of me not to include an extremely important topic: *toxic positivity*.

For those of you who haven't come across this term, toxic positivity is the feeling of acting happy or cheerful when you're really not feeling that way. Think of that fake happiness when people say to you things such as, "Cheer up!" or, "Don't worry, things will get better!" when something really bad happens to you. Or when you're spending a weekend with friends, and you may be feeling down and sad, but instead of telling them how you feel, you keep your feelings to yourself and pretend that everything is great.

Toxic positivity can make you inauthentic, cause you to lose touch with reality and also distance you from others. It can have harmful long-term consequences because it inhibits us from feeling perfectly normal emotions, which, if left unchecked, can lead to longer-lasting, deeper issues such as anxiety, diminished self-esteem and burnout.

Having experienced all of these issues and having to keep my mental health in check on a continuous basis, one of my biggest drivers for writing this book has been to have, in one place, all the methods and tools that can help.

All of our emotions work together as our guide for us to know when things are going well or not so well; let's think of them as a warning signal, so that we can put plans in place to deal with those emotions.

Feelings of sadness, anxiety, anger and fear are completely normal and should be shared with close friends you can rely on, family members you can trust, your GP or a health professional (I have included a list of professional organisations on page 209 in *Further Resources*, whom you can talk to about how you are feeling if you aren't comfortable talking to your family or friends); they shouldn't be kept to yourself. The more you avoid negative thoughts, the bigger they can grow. And as the saying goes: *a problem shared is a problem halved*. In the past, I haven't found this easy to do, but during the pandemic, I've realised the importance of sharing thoughts and feelings with the right loved ones.

Regarding this book, I'd like to say that I really want anyone reading it to try to be open about how you're feeling – there shouldn't be any shame or guilt.

Your notebook is a great addition here. Perhaps you could try writing down on paper how you're really feeling, ahead of speaking to somebody about it. I know personally how much writing (or journalling) can help to get thoughts, emotions and feelings out of your head.

Finally, some research[1] around toxic positivity proves that it can be extremely dangerous to cover up how you're really feeling and that too much positivity can be a bad thing. A 10-year Stanford University study[2] finds that using a coping mechanism of denying negative feelings is linked to higher levels of depression. Another study[3] in 2011 reveals that people actually feel sadder when others expect them not to feel negative emotions, such as sadness. I can totally relate to all of this, so please be kind to yourself.

Setting the scene

Firstly, congratulations! I know how hard it was to make the decision to change and that it was possibly triggered by something pretty monumental happening in your life, but let me assure you that, by you even buying this book and getting to this sentence, I know you want this badly, and just as badly as I did.

There will be myriad different scenarios you may be going through right now: a job you don't like, a boss you can't stand, a relationship that needs to end, a need to move house, rolling along on autopilot, feeling stuck and uninspired, general overwhelm, apathy, or a loss of mojo. Although this book is aimed at women in midlife (with 'midlife' meaning approximately age 40 to age 65), with or without children, it's my greatest wish that the information within this book is helpful for those of any age or gender with the very same feelings of being stuck, unsure what direction to go in next and with many dreams inside of you, ready to discover.

You aren't alone. Not only have I been through these difficult times but many others have too, and let me assure you there's a way out to a much better future, and the steps that I'm about to take you through can get you there.

I'm thankful to have discovered so many incredible inspiring individuals during the years I was experiencing this, as well as the answers I was searching for, and my life very slowly got better and better – much better than it had ever been.

It's my quest, mission and belief that this process of unravelling and getting unstuck need not take more than a year. In fact, with the right tools, knowledge, support and encouragement behind you, and the information within the pages of this book, you can transform your life into one that's fulfilled, happier, and full of potential, possibilities and opportunity.

The small, baby-step changes I made to my life worked for me, so there's no reason why they can't work for you too. Even if you think that you're too busy and have no time to fit in some of the things I talk about in this book, I include notes in the 'Time-Poor Tips' sections for ways to fit these things into your life. You'll be amazed at how much impact just 5 minutes of some of the actions within the book can have on your life, and they're already tried and tested by me, my friends and my clients.

This is most definitely *not* a 'you must do everything I tell you' book, but a companion and a guide to get you unstuck and living a better life that puts you first. Some of the ideas will resonate more than others, and I've set out as clearly as possible what the benefits of doing these things are to one's mind and body. Even if you were able to do three of the things in the first chapter on a regular basis, this would be an incredible achievement and one you should be very proud of.

Finally, this book won't explore peri- and post-menopause in any detail, which many of us in midlife may be affected by and not realise. This topic is not only complex but, at the time of writing, there are around 34 symptoms these can cause.

Big thanks goes to the inspirational Kate Oakley, my ex-colleague and friend, who at age 50 has completely changed career from the corporate world of human resources (HR) to become a personal trainer for midlife women, with a specialism in peri-/post-menopause (she did months of research). I'm now much wiser thanks to Kate, and it's good to know the basics, including that a woman is peri-menopausal until 12 months have gone by since her last period and is post-menopausal thereafter.

Kate's advice is to do your research; start tracking your symptoms; refer to the website of Dr Louise R. Newson, the 'Menopause Doctor', general practitioner (GP) and menopause specialist; have a look at Alva (Understand Your Menopause); and finally, follow Cathy Proctor (@meandmyhrt) on Instagram. Dr Sarah McKay, a neuroscientist (I studied with her), recommends the book *The Menopause Manifesto, Own your health with facts and feminism*. All of the details for these individuals and this book can be found in *Further Resources* (starting on page 208).

So, let's begin. I'll first introduce to you 'the elixir of life': *the mighty motivation magic hormones.*

The mighty motivation magic hormones

There are some very clever chemicals released into the bloodstream that influence our happiness, and they can have a fundamental and mostly positive impact on our mental health, mood, productivity, behaviour, physiology and emotions.

I was towards the end of writing this book when I realised I needed to include details of the very magical hormones that can be released when you apply the positive things outlined in the following chapters. I recognised that, when you combine these different activities, you then produce a cocktail of different hormones, which have the potential to supercharge your life.

I've seen the changes first-hand in myself and others, so I know their power! **The names of these hormones are as follows:**

* Dopamine

* Oxytocin

* Serotonin

* Endorphins

* Melatonin

So as not to blind you with too much science so early on, these hormones are detailed in the *Appendix* on page 215. In my summaries for each of the steps in the first few chapters, I include which hormones are involved with what activity. You can find this in the sections titled 'Mighty Motivation Magic Hormones'.

> *"If you want things to change, you have to change. If you will change, everything will change for you."*
>
> – Jim Rohn

The five steps to motivation magic that can supercharge your life

When I was asked to do a talk about what keeps me motivated, the acronym SEWPA was born:

1. **S** stands for 'self-care' (or 'self-development')
2. **E** stands for 'environment'
3. **W** stands for 'why'
4. **P** stands for 'planning'
5. **A** stands for 'assistance'

All of these terms will be explained in the next chapter, but excitingly, I was then able to use the play on words with SEWPA sounding like 'super' and then 'charge your life'. Get it? Because all of these things supercharged my life, so now it's time for you to try them too and supercharge *your* life! In the following chapters, you'll notice I've explained in detail the background of each element, and sometimes, the science or neuroscience and research behind it. If you're short on time, my advice is to skip to the sections headed 'Recap'; each of these will give you a good overview of the topic in question.

So here it is, the secret sauce, the elixir of life, the motivation magic and the ingredients that – if done consistently on a daily or at least a regular basis – can literally change your life. So hang on to your seat – here we go!

"A little progress each day adds up to big results."

– Satya Nani

CHAPTER ONE

STEP 1: SELF-CARE

'Self-care' means so many different things to different people, but Lexico (formerly Oxford Dictionaries online) explains it as being "the practice of taking action to preserve or improve one's own health" and "the practice of taking an active role in protecting one's own well-being and happiness, in particular during periods of stress".[4] These days, when people talk about self-care, they generally mean the conscious and deliberate choice to do something that looks after you and your well-being.

When I meet my clients and also look back to the beginning of my transformation journey, the number-one thing I see that we need to address first is to take a look at ourselves and how we manage our lives. You'll notice that this chapter is the longest, because nurturing and caring for ourselves is what we need to spend time on first, and this makes the other chapters in the book easier to tackle. Consider it to be putting all the fundamentals in place to give you a solid, supportive structure with the tools and strategies to then move towards changing your life, unlocking potential, and opening up possibilities and opportunities for you.

Running on autopilot, not putting yourself first, being constantly stressed, feeling burnt out, not looking after your health and not finding the time for exercise – you'll probably recognise most, if not all, of these. But don't worry, you can change all of that...

In this section, I'll be covering the following:

✓ **Morning magic routine** – *Start your day in the right way with a morning routine:*

* Hydrate, hydrate, hydrate

* Mindfulness meditation

* Affirmations – Make it true

* Exercise – Medicine for your mind and body

* Visualisation – See your future

* Gratitude – Change the way you think

✓ **Daytime magic routine** – *Continue your day in the right way:*

* Learning – Open your mind

* Reading – Reading is to your mind what exercise is to your body

* YouTube videos and TED (technology, entertainment, design) talks – The big motivators

* Listening to podcasts – Take your mind off that mindless chore

* Nutrition – You are what you eat

* Clothes – You are what you wear

* Mobile phones – Love them or hate them?

* The to-do list – Why a list of three things really works

* Sleep – The great healer
* Emotional freedom technique (EFT) – Reduce stress and anxiety fast

Morning magic routine

Start your day in the right way with a morning routine

Before I began this journey, self-care had never factored into my life. In fact, I don't remember ever having come across the term. Furthermore, having suffered from burnout and recovered, I wasn't really aware that self-care was a thing.

What I did realise, however, was that having me time was important, whether it was taking 5 minutes out to read a book, walk round the block, meditate, spend time with friends, exercise, learn something new or just sit quietly for a few moments of contemplation.

In June 2017, I discovered an incredible book that went on to radically change my life: *The Miracle Morning* by Hal Elrod.[5] This wonderful book is all about creating an experience of waking up feeling energised and excited, and doing it on a daily basis for the rest of your life.

Creating a morning routine can help you feel calm, controlled and powerful, and it can set the tone for your entire day. It may mean the difference between a productive or a sluggish one, by having a powerful ripple effect on your mood, happiness and focus. If you leave it to chance, you'll likely get side-tracked by distractions and other people's priorities, and then find yourself consumed by stress.

Picking up your mobile phone to scroll through your emails or social media the minute you wake up will create information overload by hitting you with too much stimulation before you're fully awake, and it will interfere with your ability to prioritise tasks, making for a far-less-productive day!

Let's go back to Hal's book. At age 20, Hal was hit head on by a drunk driver whose vehicle was travelling at 70 mph; he broke 11 bones, was dead for 6 minutes, and his parents were told by the doctors that if he ever came out of his coma, he would have permanent brain damage and may never walk again. He defied all odds and – through sheer positivity, grit and determination – walked again and fully recovered.

When he went back to work, Hal suffered from a bout of depression and developed his SAVERS (silence, affirmations, visualisation, exercise, reading and scribing) morning routine. This habit inspired me to lose three dress sizes, run a half-marathon and exercise daily; I've continued my daily routine to this day.

I've adapted his routine to form what I now called my 'mighty morning magic routine'.

I'm excited to take you through this process!

Hydrate, hydrate, hydrate

If you consider that the brain is 70–85% water, it's not surprising that we get brain fog sometimes when we haven't drunk enough. Not only does water make up more than two-thirds of our body weight, but without it, we'd die within a few days. A mere 2% drop in our body's supply can trigger signs of dehydration, such as poor short-term memory. During the night, we can also lose up to 1 litre due to sweating.

So, for that reason and on Hal's recommendation, the first thing I do once the alarm has gone off and I've got out of bed is to drink two large glasses of water while making coffee. While writing this book, I've been adding to my water a capful of Willy's Live Apple Cider Vinegar (which is good for your gut) and a squeeze of lemon for taste; add whatever makes it easy for you, as I know water isn't everybody's favourite!

My cousin Lucy is one of those cool cousins: she was married to the guitarist of Wang Chung, a 1980s pop band. I always remember her saying that her trick for looking so young (at least 10 years younger than her real age) was drinking hot water and lemon every morning for the last 30 odd years; as a result, I think of her most mornings and of all the good it's doing to my skin and body.

Leave 30 minutes between drinking lemon and brushing your teeth, however, as it's better for your oral health.[6]

When you drink water on an empty stomach, you'll flush out harmful toxins, leaving your body fresh and healthy. Drinking plenty of water can help to increase the production of muscle cells and new blood cells. It also prevents brain fog, increases clarity, prevents headaches, reduces body odour, aids digestion and makes us less constipated, makes us less hungry, improves our mood and energy levels, reduces water retention, and creates glowing skin.

Just be careful not to overdose on water, as that can also be dangerous; up to 1.5 litres a day is a good amount for women and 2 litres for men.[7]

Recap: Drink two large glasses of water when you wake up, to hydrate your body and brain; herbal teas are just as good.

Facts: Dehydration leads to fatigue because it impacts the flow of oxygen to the brain and causes your heart to work harder to pump oxygen to all your bodily organs, making you more tired and less alert. By staying hydrated, you stay energised. According to one study,[8] thirsty participants who drank water before performing cognitive tasks reacted faster than people who didn't drink water beforehand.

Benefits: Your focus and concentration are improved, and your energy levels are boosted! There are plenty of benefits from drinking lemon and water: it's a good source of vitamin C, which boosts your immune system; it improves your skin quality; it's good for digestion; and it helps to flush toxins out of your body by cleansing the liver, which then helps to fend off bloating and offers detox benefits.

Top Tips: Use a Brita filter to make your water pure. Add a squeeze and a slice of lemon or lime, frozen berries or mint. Herbal teas also count as water or use fresh mint – all delicious! Keep an eye on the colour of your pee during the day, as it's a good indication of dehydration: it should be a nice, light straw colour. Carry a water bottle with you during the day as it'll remind you to drink.

Time-Poor Tips: Take a glass of water to bed at night and drink it when you wake up. Drink another glass of water while you're waiting for the kettle to boil. Fill a litre bottle in the morning and drink it throughout the day.

Budget Friendly Tips: Water from the tap is free.

"Water is the driving force in nature."

– Leonardo da Vinci

Mindfulness meditation

The Cambridge Dictionary definition of 'mindfulness' is "the practice of being aware of your body, mind, and feelings in the present moment, thought to create a feeling of calm"[9] and its definition of 'meditation' is "the act of giving your attention to only one thing, either as a religious activity or as a way of becoming calm and relaxed".[10]

It's so good for you in so many different ways! Treat yourself and go back to bed for this bit. Bed is one of my favourite places in the world, and there's nothing better than drinking coffee and then meditating somewhere super comfortable and cosy.

In March 2017, I lost a very dear friend of mine – Francesca Sheldon – to mental illness. I think of Francesca a lot, particularly as she was the one who told me to try meditation when I was going through a particularly difficult time. When she mentioned it, I remember thinking that it was woo-woo and a load of old nonsense, and so I didn't take her advice at the time, but I've come to realise how right she was in more ways than one!

In one day, a human being can produce 60,000–80,000 thoughts. That's an average of 2,500–3,300 thoughts per hour. *Isn't that incredible?* The mind is like a butterfly that flies from one flower to another, never standing still. Sometimes, this endless flow of thoughts is tiring and exhausting, especially when you're anxious or worried. The magic of meditation is that it slows down the stream of thinking and enables your mind to become calm and peaceful. Your mind is then more able to focus, and it works better at solving problems, making plans, studying and working.

When you become aware of your thoughts and pay attention, you'll be amazed to discover that most thoughts are unimportant, and according to research conducted by the National Science Foundation,[11] around 80% of them are negative. *How amazing is that?* These thoughts could be words you repeat in your mind, comments the mind makes, repeating what you've heard said, questions, answers or a lot of senseless wandering that you might not even be aware of nor are doing you any good, especially if they're negative! This explains why mindfulness meditation is so good for us, and it's such a simple tool that we can use to calm ourselves down at any point in the day and switch off those damaging negative notions that have been programmed into our minds since birth.

There are many books, YouTube videos and apps (such as Calm, Headspace and Insight Timer) on how to meditate, which can guide you through the process. I've included my favourites in the *Further Resources* section on pages 212–213.

Headspace, the world-renowned meditation app, states that 5 minutes spent practising a guided meditation, unguided meditation or visualisation imagery is proven to improve focus, self-compassion, mood, immune function and quality of sleep.[12]

I usually use one of these apps, or I google "meditation videos" and type in how I want to feel (such as energised, calm or happy) or what's resonating on that particular day. For example, if I want to feel energised, I type in "energy meditation 5 minutes" or similar, depending on how much time I have.

I'd say it's worth investing in a good meditation teacher. I've discovered and worked with Anneke Thordsen (see page 210 in *Further Resources* for contact details), who comes highly recommended. She teaches how to meditate properly, with all the ins and outs.

For those of us who don't get on with meditating – and it doesn't suit everybody – you could try alternatives such as hiking, dancing, exercising, playing with pets or knitting, which are all other possible activities that bring your attention to the present moment.

Recap: Build meditation into your morning routine; start by trying 5 minutes and see how you go. If you're already meditating, then that's fantastic! Use an app or google a meditation for how you want to feel that day.

Facts: Researchers at Johns Hopkins University analysed 47 trials (which included over 3,500 people);[13] they conclude that mindfulness meditation programmes can help reduce anxiety. In 2011, Sara Lazar and her team at Harvard identified that mindfulness meditation can actually change the structure of the brain: eight weeks of mindfulness-based stress reduction (MBSR) was found to increase cortical thickness in the hippocampus, which governs learning and memory.[14]

Benefits: Meditating is a great way to focus your mind, relax, improve your attention, increase your sense of well-being, boost your creativity, improve your memory and reduce pain (physical and emotional); there are many other benefits as well.

Top Tips: First thing in the morning or last thing at night are great times to meditate. Either lie down in bed, or sit in your favourite chair or on the sofa – placing your feet flat on the floor gets you grounded.

Time-Poor Tips: Even 5 minutes of meditation daily is beneficial. Use one of the apps if you're out for a walk, or try 5 or 10 minutes of mindfulness. What can you see? What can you hear? What can you smell? What are you feeling?

Budget Friendly Tips: Videos and audio online are free, as are the various apps mentioned in the back of this book.

Mighty Motivation Magic Hormones: Serotonin, endorphins and reduced cortisol.

"Watch your thoughts; they become words. Watch your words; they become actions. Watch your actions; they become habit. Watch your habits; they become character. Watch your character; it becomes your destiny."

– Lao Tzu

Affirmations – Make it true

So what does 'affirmation' mean and what do they actually do? The Cambridge Dictionary definitions are "a statement or sign that something is true", "the act of saying yes or of showing that you mean yes", and finally, "support or approval".[15]

When we repeat a statement to ourselves that we want to be true, we start to believe it over time because our subconscious can't distinguish between the truth and a lie. That statement then becomes our reality. For example, if you tell yourself over and over again that you're scared of snakes, this then becomes your reality, and soon, whenever you see a snake, you'll feel really afraid. You've told your brain you're afraid of something, so your brain causes your body to react with fear.

According to research by Dr David Eagleman, a neurologist and best-selling author featured in *The Nature of Things* documentary, 95% of our decisions are made by our unconscious mind.[16]

Something is said to be subconscious when it's beneath your consciousness. You're still awake and perceiving the outside world, but there's something beneath or beyond your consciousness that's influencing you.

The conscious mind is the part of the mind that is responsible for rationalising, paying attention, logical thinking and reasoning. For example, if a person is asked to add 25 and 25, it's the conscious mind that will work out the calculation and give the answer.

However, the subconscious mind is responsible for all the involuntary actions and accessible information that are received in our day-to-day lives. For example, the continuous processes of breathing, blood circulation and heart beating are known to be controlled by an individual's subconscious mind, as are our emotions. The subconscious mind is also perceived to be the place where individual beliefs, attitudes and memories are stored.

A subconscious negative feeling you have towards a type of food might be the result of getting sick from it as a child, which you've since forgotten. Something that's subconscious is usually passive, and you aren't actively thinking about it.

When we repeat positive affirmations to ourselves, we essentially train our brains to believe that thing. If you tell yourself over and over again, "I'm confident," you'll soon start to feel more confident.

I've used affirmations for a number of years now with very positive results. Instead of saying, "I can't do this," or "I don't feel confident," I started to repeat affirmations such as, "I can do anything I put my mind to," and, "I am so happy and grateful that I am now living an incredible life full of fun, excitement and adventures," and my confidence and self-esteem slowly returned.

If I was travelling anywhere in my car, and I was feeling particularly out of my comfort zone, I'd speak different affirmations out loud. By the time I got to my destination, I'd be feeling so much better. The positive energy that you create by speaking them out loud with enthusiasm really makes a difference, and speaking them aloud really helped me!

As a small-business owner, I spent many months struggling doing things on my own until I started using the affirmation, "I am able to let go and let people help me." Because I've told myself that it's going to happen, it's now a belief. That belief has become my reality.

Use this affirmation for a few weeks and see what happens: "I am able to let go and let people help me."

The formula for writing effective affirmations is quite simple:

1. Effective affirmations are written in the first person; for example, "I am...," etc.

2. Affirmations are written in the positive (as opposed to the negative); for example, "I am feeling happy."

3. Affirmations have an emotional charge. When you say them out loud, it's important to put feeling and emotion into them, otherwise it's a waste of time.

4. Affirmations are written in the present tense, as if it has already happened. Here are some great examples:

    *   "I have sky-high self-esteem."

    *   "I am thankful for my wonderful future."

* "I am able to make unlimited income flow into my life."
* "I create my life with my vision."
* "I love my healthy lifestyle."
* "I am so grateful for my excellent memory."
* "I have limitless creative potential."
* "I can do anything I set my mind to."

Recap: People use affirmations for a variety of purposes. Generally speaking, affirmations are used to reprogram the subconscious mind, and to encourage us to believe certain things about ourselves or about the world and our place within it. They're also used to help us create the reality we want – often in terms of making (or attracting) wealth, love, beauty and happiness.

Facts: Affirmations are simply statements that are designed to create self-change in the individual using them. They can serve as inspiration, as well as simple reminders. They also can serve to focus your attention on goals throughout the day, which has the potential, in and of itself, to promote positive and sustained self-change.

Benefits: Changing the way you think about yourself and the world – essentially your thoughts and feelings – from a negative stance to a positive one can only be a good thing!

Top Tips: Write affirmations on Post-Its and place them on your mirror, laptop, computer, fridge or pinboard (I have them typed up on an A4 piece of paper, which I've laminated), and say them aloud, say them with feeling and emotion, and believe what you're saying. Car journeys on your own are fantastic opportunities to say affirmations out loud to build confidence. Write your affirmations in a notebook, and then repeat them out loud first thing in the morning and last thing at night.

Time-Poor Tips: Carry your affirmations around with you on a card; focus on just five to start with. Keep repeating them daily. Have a list by the kettle or wherever you spend the most time, and repeat them aloud. Record yourself saying them on your phone and play back the recording in bed at night or first thing in the morning.

Budget Friendly Tips: Charity shops are good sources of cheap notepads. If you don't have a car, you can still say your affirmations out loud in the confines of your home.

Mighty Motivation Magic Hormones: Dopamine, serotonin and oxytocin.

"Affirmations are like seeds planted in soil. Poor soil, poor growth. Rich soil, abundant growth. The more you choose to think thoughts that make you feel good, the quicker the affirmations work."

– *Louise Hay*

Exercise – Medicine for your mind and body

Exercise has been one of the most important parts of my transformation. It enabled me to lose a whopping three dress sizes! In fact, it's been so fantastic for my mental health that I now call it 'my medicine'. I also believe that it may be helping me with a few menopausal symptoms (sadly, I can't prove this).

When I began my fitness journey, I started with walking, building up to a short 15-minute walk daily. Then I downloaded a couple of apps: The Scientific 7-Minute Workout and 7M Women – Workout for Women. I'd then do these 7-minute high-intensity interval training (HIIT) sessions at home, making sure I did something every day.

Over time, I became addicted to exercise and it became a habit, particularly running (thanks to the feel-good hormones of endorphins and dopamine it produces). It took about 4 months to start running (I had to lose enough weight that I could actually run), and then, like a mad thing, I booked into the Surrey Hills half-marathon to motivate me to keep going (and yes, I did complete it; it's a beautiful run/walk that I highly recommend).

My dad has always been an inspiration to me when it comes to exercise; at 87 years old (at the time of writing this book), he still manages to go for regular walks, and it's a lovely opportunity for me to spend some quality time with him, have a chat and a catch up. Research shows going for a walk can be even better for you than drinking a cup of coffee if you need an energy boost.[17,18]

Exercise is important for all sorts of reasons. It helps you to stay healthy, improves your mood, and improves your strength and stamina. Incredibly, it can also help you to learn too. Researchers at the University of British Columbia[19] have found that people who exercise regularly have a bigger brain volume in the area of the hippocampus, which is linked to learning. It also boosts the size of your prefrontal cortex and medial temporal cortex. These areas are linked to thinking and memory, so if you happen to be studying, exercise will help you to stay energised and focused.

As stated in the *Journal of Sport & Exercise Psychology*,[20] the more physically active people are, the greater their general feelings of excitement and enthusiasm: "People who were more physically active overall had higher pleasant–activated feelings than people who were less physically active, and on days when people were more physically active than was typical for them, they reported higher levels of pleasant–activated feelings."

The American College of Sports Medicine published a study[21] showing that a team of doctors has determined that taking three 30-minute brisk walks or jogs a week improves happiness and even enhances recovery from clinical depression. The results were stronger than those from studies using medication and studies using exercise and medication combined.

Group exercise may give you a significant endorphin boost. According to a small study,[22] 12 participants saw a higher endorphin boost when exercising (rowing) in a group than when they did similar exercise alone.

I know how hard it can be to get motivated to start a new fitness regime. My advice is to start small and build it up. Start with 1 minute, then 2 minutes, then build it up to 5 minutes; take a walk around the block; or do one press-up, one sit-up, etc. Also make sure it's something that you really enjoy or love. Think about what you used to love doing when you were a child or teenager. It's never too late to try again. I just tried roller skating after 37 years and I loved it just as much – it's just scarier than I remember!

It could be anything from skipping, climbing or waterskiing to Pilates or yoga. Walk up the stairs at home a few times when you need a break. Download an app (do a Google search by typing in "exercise apps"). Try a challenge with press-ups or the plank, and if you want to involve your family, you could do family exercise challenges.

One idea I read about is to play hide-and-sweat (a variation of hide-and-seek); let's call it a fitness treasure hunt. Write down activities on separate pieces of paper (for example, do 10 star jumps, do five push-ups or crawl like a snake) and hide them around the house or garden. Get your kids to seek out the clues, and when they find one, you both do the activity. Or you could set up an obstacle course in the garden, with something to crawl under, something to jump over, some things to swerve between or something to throw.

Alternatively, if you want some accountability, find an online challenge to join, as you may find it easier to do this when you're accountable to a group. You could also make yourself accountable by working one-to-one (1-2-1) with a personal trainer, or a yoga or Pilates trainer/teacher, for example.

At the time of writing this book, my routine consists of running every other day of the week (anything up to 5 kilometres), and on the other days, using the app 7M Women – Workout for Women, which consists of short 7–20 minute routines. I now also use a standing desk, which burns some calories as you work, as long as you move around constantly and also take rests.

A performance coach and exercise physiologist from the Human Performance Institute in Orlando, Florida, came up with the genius 7-minute programme: The Scientific 7-Minute Workout. They wanted to give their busy clients a more efficient, yet still effective workout, and they put together a series of 12 different exercises that work the upper body, lower body and core. Each exercise is 30 seconds long, which is enough to get in about 15 to 20 repetitions. In between sets, you rest for about 10 seconds. The 12 exercises in the 7-minute workout target all the body's major muscle groups and are a really effective all-round exercise. I love it. My wonderful friend Becky does too!

As a menopausal woman, I'm also trying to bring strength training into my routine. Thanks to Kate Oakley at Your Future Fit (as mentioned earlier), I now know that our osteoporosis risk skyrockets following menopause (oestrogen is needed to help lay down bone), so strength training is vital. Strength-training exercises will help to build bone and muscle strength, burn body fat, and rev up your metabolism.

Recap: Start small – with 5 or 7 minutes exercise, one sit-up or one press up – and build it up from there. Remember, half an hour of brisk walking or jogging three times a week improves happiness and can improve recovery from clinical depression.

Facts: As stated in a blog post by Lisa Fields in the popular MyFitnessPal app, "'The best available evidence suggests that exercise induces changes in brain neurotransmitters, which play a role in boosting energy,' explains Patrick O'Connor, PhD, a University of Georgia kinesiology professor who authored two studies on walking and the benefits. 'Likely brain norepinephrine, dopamine, serotonin or histamine is involved.'"[23]

Benefits: Exercise can improve memory and brain function (across all age groups), protect against many chronic diseases, aid weight management, lower blood pressure, improve heart health, improve your quality of sleep, reduce feelings of anxiety and depression, combat cancer-related fatigue, reduce joint pain and stiffness, improve mood, raise energy levels and increase attention levels. One Stanford University study[24] reveals that walking increases creative output by an average of 60%. That's a whopping increase for an average score!

Top Tips: Keep moving throughout the day. Invest in a standing desk; it's great, as it burns a few more calories than when you're sitting, and it has various benefits, including blood sugar levels returning to normal faster after a meal on days when a person spends a longer time standing. Furthermore, standing rather than sitting may reduce the risk of shoulder and back pain. Find an exercise you really love doing. Here are some ideas: Pilates, yoga, aerobics, roller skating, ice skating, wild swimming, walking, waterskiing, hiking, cycling, circus skills or qigong. Try to include some strength training if you're post-menopausal (an article by Katey Davidson gives the benefits of this[25]).

Time-Poor Tips: Download the 7M Women – Workout for Women app or try The Scientific 7-Minute Workout. Go for a 5-minute brisk walk. Walk up and down the stairs a few times. Build it up when you find pockets of free time. Do a few star jumps or try using a skipping rope.

Budget Friendly Tips: Exercising in your home or outdoors is completely free.

Mighty Motivation Magic Hormones: Endorphins, serotonin, dopamine and oxytocin.

> *"Strength does not come from physical capacity.*
> *It comes from an indomitable will."*
>
> *- Mahatma Gandhi*

Visualisation – See your future

Visualisation is explained well in the Cambridge Dictionary definition of the verb 'visualise': "to form a picture of someone or something in your mind, in order to imagine or remember him, her, or it".[26]

It's something I do on a regular basis using my vision board; there's more on vision boards later (see page 121 in *Chapter 3*).

Our brains don't know the difference between what we've actually done and what we've imagined. By using our senses to imagine over and over as vividly as possible what we'd like to happen in the future or how we'd like to feel, we're able to reprogram our thought and behaviour patterns.

In sports, sports coaches work with athletes using visualisation to 'intend' an outcome of a race or training session, or simply to rest in a relaxed feeling of calm and well-being. Diver Troy Dumais, a four-time Olympian, uses visualisation as a way of practising his performance mentally: "If you can see yourself hitting a dive, the chances of you hitting a dive increase greatly." I've used visualisation to achieve many things in the past; in particular, I've used it to improve my running.

Athletes use visualisation for these sorts of things:

*   to stay relaxed before or between events;

*   to achieve the proper mental state for competing;

*   to manage the physical discomfort that comes with pushing your body to its limits;

*   to increase confidence prior to an event;

* to compartmentalise errors and move past mistakes; and/
or

* to rebound after a bad event.

So how do you visualise? It helps to note your visualisation down. I keep a notebook by my bed with my vision for my future in it and what I want to happen over the year. I also use my vision board, which is a representation of what I want in pictures and words cut from magazines (see page 122 in *Chapter 3*).

I've talked about how our minds can easily flit around like a butterfly (in the 'Mindfulness meditation' section), so when you're visualising and your mind is wandering, you can simply open your eyes and reread your notes. It's good to break up your visualisation into different parts; for example, finances, relationships and work. As an example, if you want to run your own business, you see yourself as a successful person, splitting your time between working at home, going to a shared office space and going to meetings, and earning your chosen amount a month. You look forward to picking up the phone to talk to people about your amazing business, as you're helping others.

It also helps if this image really excites you! Generating the emotions and feelings of success is the key to visualising effectively. Feel proud of yourself, feel how amazing it is to be your own boss, feel confident and excited, and imagine all the money that will come into your bank account.

By using visualisation, you're training your brain to see things as you'd like them to be instead of as they are. Hal Elrod says that for 5 minutes each morning, you should "visualise living your ideal day, performing all tasks with ease, confidence and enjoyment."[27]

The key is to make the pictures in your mind as bright and vivid as you can. Really see yourself acting the way you want to be. Look around you and take in your surroundings. Where are you? Who else is there? You could maybe talk to those people (friends, family or colleagues) in your visualisation. What are they doing? What are you doing? How are you doing it? Notice all the little details. Look for additional details to make the picture clearer. What's the weather like? What are you wearing? What can you see? What can you feel? What can you smell? Take the time to notice and feel the texture of your clothes, the temperature of the room or place, and any other small details you notice.

You're effectively planting new memories into your subconscious. The most important part of visualisation is the emotional part – try to generate the same feelings and emotions that you would have if you'd already accomplished your goals. Think of the excitement and delight you'd feel on achieving something you've wanted for years and how amazing that would be! You could feel energised, joyful, proud, successful, happy, wealthy, confident, etc.

In his book *How the Mind Can Heal Your Body*, David R. Hamilton, PhD, describes how visualisation has shown positive results in spinal-injury rehabilitation, as well as in improving the movement of patients with Parkinson's disease.[28] Patients use their minds to imagine moving normally, and the moment they do so, the arm or leg that they envision in motion is stimulated. The result is that their movements improve over time, and in some stroke cases, some damaged brain areas begin to regenerate.

A blog from one of the popular meditation apps, InsightTimer (which I highly recommend using), 'How visualization can help ease anxiety' gives the details of a study by João Apostolo and Katharine Kolcaba.[29] This study investigated how guided visualisation can minimise feelings of anxiety in a clinical population. The researchers asked patients with severe anxiety to listen to a CD every day for 10 days. The CD utilised guided visualisation techniques, and the patients were invited to visualise spaces in which they felt comfortable and at ease. This included surrounding themselves with people that they love and immersing themselves in pleasant scenery. Unsurprisingly, the patients had significantly reduced anxiety scores after the 10 days.

You can visualise as often as you like – just do what feels right for you. I don't do it every morning, but usually three to five times a week for anything from about 5–20 minutes. And enjoy it!

Recap: Visualisation is when you create a picture in your mind of someone or something, in order to imagine or remember the person(s) or scene. You can practise this technique as often as you want, taking anything from 5–20 minutes at a time. Focus on a particular goal and go there in your imagination: See it, feel it, be it, do it, believe it and put yourself there.

Facts: Athletes use visualisation to boost performance, calm their nerves and achieve their best times. In some stroke victims, damaged brain areas begin to regenerate when using visualisation. Visualisation can be used as an aid for reducing anxiety.

Benefits: Visualisation is a great way to increase motivation, be clear on what you want from life, think positively and optimise your performance (it worked for me in my half-marathon!), and it reduces stress as it calms the mind.

Top Tips: You can visualise literally anywhere: on the train, at home and at work. Your mind is powerful, so keep exploring and create the life you want with the help of visualisation. At the very least it'll get you really excited about life!

Time-Poor Tips: Start with 5 minutes of visualisation once or twice a week, and then build it up if you can. Use your time on the loo to visualise, or perhaps do it when waiting for the kettle to boil, or instead of watching Netflix, Amazon Prime or TV one night a week.

Budget Friendly Tips: Visualisation is completely free. Remember, when you imagine every step of an event or activity going well, you get your mind and body ready to take those steps in real life.

Mighty Motivation Magic Hormones: Dopamine.

"Imagination is more important than knowledge. For while knowledge defines all we currently know and understand, imagination points to all we might yet discover and create."

- Albert Einstein

Gratitude – Change the way you think

Sadly, our minds have a tendency to fall victim to negativity bias. We tend to remember the events that went wrong more than the ones that went right, and we usually hang on to the negative thing our family member, friend or colleague said, and we forget the praise we received recently.

Gratitude is terrific because it shifts your attention from the negative to the positive in a really short space of time. You can simply experience a feeling of gratitude, or you can write it down, read it back and feel the emotion that comes with it. Part of my morning routine is writing out three things that I'm really grateful for. As I've already mentioned, I keep a notebook by my bed at all times so I can write notes, and it's a great medium for when I get ideas in the middle of the night.

Dr Melanie Greenberg writes, "Feeling and expressing gratitude turns our mental focus to the positive, which compensates for our brains' natural tendency to focus on threats, worries, and negative aspects of life. As such, gratitude creates positive emotions like joy, love, and contentment, which research shows can undo the grip of negative emotions like anxiety. Fostering gratitude can also broaden your thinking and create positive cycles of thinking and behaving in healthy, positive ways."[30]

Gratitude is the antidote to negativity. When you're experiencing true feelings of gratitude, there's no room for anything else. It's impossible to be grateful and angry/fearful/stressed at the same time. Being grateful is a powerful way to reduce anxiety.

Vital brain functions that affect mood, sleep, memory, learning, concentration and motor control are influenced by the levels of dopamine in a person's body. Feelings of gratitude flood our brains with dopamine (which is also released when we eat something delicious and when we have sex). This feeling is so good that we're motivated to feel it again and again, and it becomes addictive. I always wondered why when I miss my gratitude routine for a day, I really notice it!

In a study where people were asked to write three things they were grateful for every day for 10 weeks, the results show they achieved better sleep, better connections with others, greater optimism, improved happiness and a feeling of well-being.[31]

So, if this isn't part of your daily routine already, it's a helpful thing to start; plus, it only takes a couple of minutes at the most and it can be combined with journalling.

 To get you going, you could have a think about the following (and pop the answers in your notebook):

» Write about a person in your life whom you're especially grateful for right now, and why that is.

» What activities and hobbies did you miss the most during lockdown?

» What's something you're grateful to have learnt this week?

» What materialistic items are you most grateful for?

Recap: Write what you feel grateful for daily (at least three things), as this will change your perspective on the world and your life.

Facts: Gratitude shifts your attention and stimulates the hypothalamus. This is a small but important area in the centre of the brain, which plays a critical role in hormone production and helps to stimulate many vital processes in the body. It's located between the pituitary gland and the thalamus. Gratitude can boost production of the neurotransmitter serotonin and activate the brain stem to produce dopamine. Serotonin is a chemical that has a wide variety of functions in the human body. It's sometimes called the 'happy chemical' because it contributes to well-being and happiness. On the other hand, dopamine plays a part in controlling the movements a person makes, as well as their emotional responses. The right balance of dopamine is vital for both physical and mental well-being.

Benefits: Gratitude creates positive emotions such as joy, love and contentment; it turns our mental focus to the positive; and it reduces stress. A 5-minutes-a-day gratitude journal can increase your long-term well-being by over 10%. You can't be grateful and angry/fearful/stressed concurrently. Being grateful is a formidable method of reducing anxiety.

Top Tips: I'd highly recommend a book called *The 6-Minute Diary*, which includes a daily space to write statements beginning with "I'm grateful for..."[32] This book is more than just a diary and has proved to be a real hit with me and many others I've recommended it to. You can read the thousands of great reviews on Amazon. Or you could keep your own notebook or daily journal of three things you're thankful or grateful for; it works well to do this first thing in the morning or just before you go to bed. Make it a practice to tell a spouse, partner or friend something you appreciate about them every day.

Time-Poor Tips: If you've no time for anything else, I'd prioritise this action of writing three things you're grateful for every day; it really is a huge gamechanger! It takes around 1 minute to do, and you should really feel the gratitude when you write each statement. Or you could type into YouTube "5 minute gratitude meditation" and take your pick of the videos that come up, like I did this morning!

Budget Friendly Tips: You can speak your gratitude out loud. Charity shops are great for finding cheaper notebooks to write down what you're grateful for daily.

Mighty Motivation Magic Hormones: Serotonin, dopamine and oxytocin.

"This is a wonderful day. I've never seen this one before."

- Maya Angelou

Daytime magic routine

Continue your day in the right way

Learning – Open your mind

Education has been widely documented by researchers as the single variable tied most directly to improved health and longevity.[33] As we get older, it's important to find things to learn and do that light up our lives. I've really grown to love learning and can't get enough of it. I try my best to factor some kind of learning into every day, whether it's reading a page from a book, listening to a podcast, watching a YouTube video or TED (technology, entertainment, design) talk, doing a challenge, or studying or doing a course.

Your brain never stops growing. Throughout a person's lifetime, the brain is continually reshaping itself in response to what it learns.

Learning is essential to our existence. Just like food nourishes our bodies, information and continued learning nourishes our minds. Lifelong learning is also an indispensable tool for every career and organisation. There are some of us who have the self-motivation and persistence to keep educating ourselves. Right now, my great love is anything self-development related, and fiction has taken a back seat.

I've recently studied to complete two certificates,[I] both of which are fantastic, but not before I spent a couple of years

---

I Neuroscience & Brain Health Certificate with The Neuroscience Academy, and a Diploma in Neuro-Linguistic Programming (NLP) with The Academy of Coaching & Training, through which I became a certified NLP practitioner and coach.

working out what I really wanted to invest time and money in to study. It couldn't be just any course; I knew that the courses would have to be super interesting, short and intensive study, as I know perfectly well that I get bored and distracted very easily, so I needed something that was going to keep me on track and interested enough to finish the course and qualify.

The main advice I'll give you if you're thinking of doing a course or studying something you love is to be realistic with yourself about how you like to study. Perhaps you find it easy to work on your own and are self-motivated, but I knew that having a group to study with and doing intensive study was the only thing that was going to work for me. Also, do your research on the courses and get recommendations too.

We're so spoilt for choice; knowledge is at our fingertips in the form of hundreds of courses available online (and offline). One of my favourite mantras – "it is never too late to do what you love" – fits well here. Expanding your skill set can help you to develop amazing new future opportunities and provide possibilities that may not have been available to you before, giving you a chance to reach your full potential.

Learning is also beneficial because it leaves you with a feeling of accomplishment that boosts your confidence in your abilities. It gives you an opportunity to step out of your comfort zones and could potentially lead to taking on a new job opportunity. It can open your mind and change your attitude by building on what you already know. The more you learn, the better you'll get at seeing additional sides of the same situation, helping you understand things more deeply.

As I mentioned earlier, we all learn in very different ways. Learning styles – also known as our 'representational systems' in the neuro-linguistic programming (NLP) world – determine how we learn. To explain NLP in greater detail, it empowers, enables and teaches us to better understand the way our brain (neuro) processes the words we use (linguistic), and how that can impact on our past, present and future (programming). It gives us strategies for observing human behaviour and learning from the best (and worst) of that! All you need is a desire to change and a willingness to learn new ways of being with yourself, with your thoughts and with others.

The main types of learning style are these:

» **Auditory:** Auditory learners enjoy lectures, seminars, audio books, podcasts and listening to music while studying. They need to hear information delivered in entertaining ways and variable tones. They will frequently create songs about information to help them remember, and they learn best when information is reinforced through sound. Fewer of our population are auditory learners; however, due to being in the digital age, a higher number of children need to think and process thoughts, and are becoming 'auditory digital' learners.

» **Kinaesthetic:** This kind of learning could involve doing experiments or role playing, and this is the tactile style of learning in which people remember information easier when performing an activity. These learners may need to wriggle or move to improve information retention.

» **Visual:** Visual learners learn best when reading or through seeing demonstrations, graphs, flow charts and brain maps. This style of learning associates information with images.

» **Reading/writing:** Students who work best in the reading/writing modality demonstrate a strong learning preference for the written word. This could include written information presented in the form of both handouts and PowerPoint slides . This modality also lends itself to conducting research online, as many information-rich sources on the internet are relatively text-heavy. Reading/writing-oriented students should be encouraged to take notes during classroom lectures to help them both process information and have an easier time recalling it later.

At the end of the day, learning should be enjoyable, so find what works best for you and the learning conditions that support and are most beneficial to you.

Finally, here are a few suggestions of different ways you can learn other than doing a course:

✓ Schedule time in your diary for learning something new from a book, research paper or online – try just 5 minutes in the morning or reading a few pages.

✓ Read online articles and magazines.

✓ Read a blog post from somebody you admire or somebody totally new to you.

✓ Subscribe to a magazine you haven't read before (I love *Positive News*, for instance).

✓ Join an association or networking group.

✓ Ask your network questions.

✓ Teach somebody else something.

✓ Discover your local library or museum; what could you learn about where you live?

✓ Apply what you've learnt.

✓ Listen to a podcasts.

There are plenty of course providers out there; my favourites include Coursera, Udemy, LinkedIn Learning, Commune, Mindvalley and Discoco.

Recap: Just like food nourishes our bodies, learning nourishes our minds. Find something you love, learn about it and then teach somebody else about it (that's what I'm doing with this book, so it's all in one place!) Your brain never stops growing. Throughout a person's lifetime, the brain is continually reshaping itself in response to what it learns.

Facts: When you're learning, important changes take place in your brain, including the creation of new connections between your neurons. This phenomenon is called 'neuroplasticity'. The more you practise, the stronger these connections become.

Benefits: Learning keeps your mind engaged and your body active. It helps you acquire new knowledge-based perspectives on the world around you. It helps you gain fresh experiences, trains your brain to handle a wide range of challenges and keeps your neural pathways active. All these factors combine to keep you healthy.

Top Tips: Be curious, and explore different topics that may stretch you but still interest and excite you. Reflect on what you've learnt, keep learning and keep loving it.

Time-Poor Tips: Book on to an online course and do one module a day, or if the module is long, split it over a week and take notes as you go.

Budget Friendly Tips: Use your local library, use the free or low-cost course platform Coursera, or type "free courses" into Google – there are many to choose from.

Mighty Motivation Magic Hormones: Serotonin, oxytocin, endorphins and dopamine.

"Intellectual growth should commence at birth and only cease at death."

- Albert Einstein

Reading – Reading is to your mind what exercise is to your body

In the very wise words of Jim Kwik, world expert in speed-reading, memory improvement, and optimal brain performance: "reading gives you an incomparable level of mental exercise, and the brain is always a 'muscle' that gets stronger the more you challenge it."[34]

When I was growing up (in lovely, leafy Chiswick), I spent my weekends in the library. I loved books so much, but as I grew older and had less time, the less I read – and when I did read, it was fiction. I have included my top-three fiction recommendations in *Further Resources* (on page 209).

When I embarked on my self-development journey at the beginning of 2017, I didn't have a TV to distract me, nor did I have young children to look after or home school! This enabled me to start reading again after about a 5-year break, but this time, self-development books replaced fiction, and I ended up reading *The Secret* by Rhonda Byrne followed by *The Miracle Morning* by Hal Elrod and many others since. My favourites include *Everything is Figureoutable* by Marie Forleo, *Vivid Vision* by Cameron Herold, *Why We Sleep* by Dr Matthew Walker and many others (see pages 208-209 in *Further Resources* for these and my other book recommendations).

Hal Elrod's advice is to read a book that will teach you or develop you in some way (self-growth/development) for 10–15 minutes every day,[35] but I just try to read a couple of pages in the morning, usually for 5 minutes. Whatever you can fit into your day, either morning or evening, is great as an alternative to TV, Netflix or Amazon Prime.

When we read, not only are we improving our memory and empathy but research has shown that it makes us feel better and more positive too. A *Blinkist* magazine article details how reading – whether it's reading a physical book or listening to an audiobook – has some amazing health benefits, including helping with depression, cutting stress and reducing the chances of developing Alzheimer's disease later in life.[36]

If reading doesn't really float your boat, then you could try any of the following:

* Listening to an audiobook or audio course.

* Reading a book from a different genre and reading for short bursts.

* Join a book club.

* Storytelling; read aloud with a friend to make it more fun.

* Attend a book festival/fair. (I love book festivals. Have a look in your area, or here are some examples: Cambridge Literary Festival, Hay Festival and Guildford Book Festival.)

* The Blinkist app summarises books for you and is so much easier to read.

Recap: Try to fit at least 5 minutes' reading in to your day, either via an e-reader, or a physical book, magazine or newspaper. Alternatively, listen to an audiobook (such as via Audible).

Facts: American sociologists argue that children who've learnt to read by the age of eight have fewer chances of being imprisoned in the future.[37] The *Harry Potter* series is one of the world's bestselling book series.

Benefits: Studies have shown that regular reading improves brain connectivity, increases your vocabulary and comprehension, empowers you to empathise with other people, aids in sleep readiness, reduces stress, lowers blood pressure and heart rate, fights depression symptoms, prevents cognitive decline as you age, and contributes to a longer life.[38] Reading boosts analytical thinking, helps us appreciate others and can be very therapeutic.

Top Tips: Schedule time to read in your diary, and make your space comfortable and enjoyable. Have a notebook with you to take notes if you like. Books make fantastic gifts. Read books that inspire you. If you don't like reading, try an audiobook instead or try storytelling with a friend.

Time-Poor Tips: Read only one paragraph, one page or one chapter, or time yourself and read for 5 minutes.

Budget Friendly Tips: Visit your local library. Charity shops are a great source of cheap books or check on Facebook Marketplace.

Mighty Motivation Magic Hormones: Oxytocin and dopamine.

"The best investment you'll ever make is in yourself.
Never stop exploring, learning, experiencing,
and becoming a better person each day."

– *Mo Seetubtim*

YouTube videos and TED talks – The big motivators

While writing this book, I've come to the realisation that I really love YouTube videos and TED talks, and they've been so valuable, helpful and motivational to me during my self-development journey and recovery.

When I had lost my mojo and felt really, really low, in a total funk, I remembered that I'd type into Google "how can I find my mojo" or "how can I get motivated and excited about life again", and then YouTube would come up with these amazing videos or TED talks that would literally save me that day from the depths of sadness and despair. It's even more wonderful that all my viewing history is saved, so I can see what I was watching and when.

YouTube was originally designed to be a dating site; however, that aspect failed, but its video-uploading prowess made it a success for that alone. Google bought YouTube for $1.65 billion in 2006, just a year and a half after it launched. Now, we all have access to millions of videos on everything from make-up tutorials to meditations.

If you haven't come across TED talks before, they're 'only good science' global talks (each a maximum of 18 minutes' long) that are inspirational, educational, diversified, emotional, powerful, surprising, engaging and very addictive. TED and TEDx talks are a must-watch if you're a visual learner. I include my favourites in *Further Resources* (on page 213) at the back of this book.

Viewers retain 95% of a video's message in comparison to 10% retention when reading the text. And the stronger the impact the video has on a viewer's emotions, the higher the level of entertainment. This is an important fact for all of us business owners to remember for our businesses!

Recap: Type into Google what you want to know plus "YouTube" and/or "TED", and you'll get a myriad of videos to choose from that will educate, motivate and fascinate you.

Facts: Every minute, over 500 hours of video are uploaded to YouTube. YouTube has over 2 billion users at the time of writing, which is almost one-third of all people on the internet. The first YouTube video was uploaded in April 2005 and it features its co-founder Jawed Karim at the San Diego Zoo. YouTube was founded by three former employees of PayPal.

The subjects of technology, entertainment and design – from which the acronym TED is derived – are three broad areas that are collectively shaping our world. Most people need visual aids to learn, and they retain far more information that way (as mentioned earlier in this section), which could be the main reason why video is better than text. Plus, a viewer is entertained more by a video that has a more profound impact.

Benefits: Watching video makes learning effective and engaging, reduces cognitive overload, and maximises retention. It also provides a cost-effective training approach, plus a simpler and more practical learning experience.

Top Tips: My top video recommendations, for those videos that motivated me in challenging times, are in *Further Resources* (on pages 213-214).

Time-Poor Tips: Swap Netflix, Amazon Prime or TV once a week with an interesting talk instead.

Budget Friendly Tips: These online videos are free to watch.

Mighty Motivation Magic Hormones: Oxytocin and dopamine.

Listening to podcasts – Occupy your mind while doing that mindless chore

I only started listening to podcasts a couple of years ago, and as with YouTube videos and TED talks, I've grown to love them very much. At the time of writing this book, I've been deliberating whether I should start my own podcast, but first things first: I needed to complete this book and then I can think about potentially doing a podcast next.

The Cambridge Dictionary definition of 'podcast' is "a digital audio file made available on the internet for downloading to a computer or mobile device, typically available as a series, new instalments of which can be received by subscribers automatically".[39]

You may or may not be an avid podcast listener, but as a reminder, podcasts are all of your favourite blogs, shows and topics (some you didn't even know you'd enjoy!) wrapped up in a huge hub of recordings (Apple Podcasts, etc.) that you can explore, download and listen to in your own time: in the car, at work, at home, working out or anywhere else. If you can google it, there's probably a podcast about it!

A 2016 study conducted at the University of California, Berkeley concludes that listening to narrative stories, similar to podcasts, can stimulate multiple parts of your brain.[40] So, whether you're looking for that adrenaline rush you get from true-crime podcasts or a comedy podcast that boosts your endorphins, there's something available for everyone.

A lovely guy called David Harris – aka Magicman London, a brilliant magician – came to one of my workshops in June 2020, and his desire to start a podcast ended up on his vision board. He then went on to create, produce and publish a weekly podcast.

You can find the *Magic Talks* podcast on all the usual platforms. (David also happens to have a very inspiring story about why and how he became a magician. I'll get him to talk about it on a podcast episode – now I have to do it!)

Recap: Podcasts are free entertainment that can be listened to anywhere through your mobile phone, laptop or PC, and they consist of conversations and stories.

Facts: A podcast is an episodic series of spoken-word digital audio files that a user can download to a personal device for easy listening. Around 40% of the UK population in the 26–35 age group listen to podcasts on a weekly basis. As of 2020, there were over 15 million podcast listeners in the UK. The audience is growing steadily as the popularity of podcasts increases, with forecasts predicting close to 20 million listeners by 2024.[41]

Benefits: Podcasts are convenient, easy to consume and a good way to learn on the go. They're free educational material, and are time-efficient, portable, and can be a way of promoting yourself and your business.

Top Tips: Listening to a podcast can be a brilliant thing to do when you have a mindless chore to complete, such as washing up or cleaning.

Time-Poor Tips: Listen while on the move, walking the dog or driving in the car.

Budget Friendly Tips: Podcasts are free to listen to.

Mighty Motivation Magic Hormones: Oxytocin and dopamine.

Nutrition – You are what you eat

I'm an absolute self-confessed foodie; a cheeseaholic with a splash of redwineaholic, though not so much these days. I love food and really enjoy eating, and I've struggled to keep the weight off in the last 15 years. Stressful jobs and sitting eating lunch at my desk didn't help, but that all really changed in 2009. I had the pleasure of meeting and working with an amazing woman who is now a very good friend: Jennifer Harper-Deacon.

Jennifer is a very talented naturopath, an award-winning journalist who was the columnist for 'What's the Alternative?' for *The Sunday Times Style* magazine, and an accomplished author, nutritionist, herbalist, acupuncturist and healer; her patients will travel long distances to see her. She has the unique gift of making people better using her incredible set of skills, including cutting-edge, evidence-based functional medicine.

I worked with her for a wonderful year, and that year totally changed my attitude towards what I put inside my body and outside my body. She taught me loads, including the importance of vitamin supplements, particularly vitamin D, as well as the risks around parabens found in personal-care and household products,[42] although there are now many paraben-free products available on the market that have been introduced over the last 12 years. Parabens can act like the hormone oestrogen in the body and disrupt the normal function of hormone systems, affecting male and female reproductive-system functioning, reproductive development, fertility and birth outcomes. Some scientists are concerned about the public's exposure to this, because the chemicals can interfere with the body's hormones and lead to health problems such as reproductive disorders, thyroid disease, asthma and cancers.

I've carried with me what I learnt over that year to today; I have continued with my daily supplements and paraben-free products, and I usually start my day off, after water and coffee, with either a smoothie or some kind of green juice. I do try my best to eat as healthily as possible and I try to avoid processed foods. Although, yes, I do have treats; we have to have treats in our lives (my guilty pleasure is Ferrero Rocher – I love them!)

I find a great person to refer to these days is Dr Rangan Chatterjee, who's regarded as one of the most influential doctors in the UK. He has been practising as a GP for 20 years, and he inspires people to transform their health and happiness through making small, sustainable changes to their lifestyles. I recommend his podcast *Feel Better, Live More* and his amazing TED talk 'How to make diseases disappear'. My great friend Clarence Pegrum introduced me to him (thank you, Clarence), and we went together to his talk where he was promoting his book *Feel Better in 5*.

So, to refer to something he wrote in his previous book, *The 4 Pillar Plan: How to Relax, Eat, Move and Sleep Your Way to a Longer, Healthier Life*, his advice is this:[43]

* De-normalise sugar (and retrain your taste buds).

* Eat five different-coloured vegetables every day.

* Eat all of your food within a 12-hour window.

* Drink eight glasses of water per day.

* Unprocess your diet by avoiding any food product that contains more than five ingredients.

This is all sensible advice that most of us know we need to do, but it's not always easy to stick to it. His point about avoiding food products that contain over five ingredients is interesting; I must think about that when I'm next buying chorizo! Note to self and to my readers: have a look at the list of ingredients. Damn, it's so delicious too!

The foods that we eat impact our well-being, not just on a cellular level but on a whole-life level: how we feel, how much energy we have, how strong we are and how capable we can be.

At this point, I also want to mention another friend, Helen Morton, who has just published her first book *Eat Well Run Strong*, which is all about nutrition for runners. Coincidentally, Helen has used the wonderful Alexa Whitten as her coach to help her write and publish this book – the same coach who I've used. Helen's book is a plethora of useful information for female runners, including the best foods for training, the impact of female hormones, and the interactions between genetics, exercise and food.[44]

Recap: You are what you put inside your body and outside your body. People are all unique. Subtle differences in genetics, body type, physical activity and environment can affect which type of diet and lifestyle you should follow. The Mediterranean diet has been ranked the best for overall health by experts for four years in a row.[45]

Facts: In his book *Feel Better in 5*, Dr Rangan Chatterjee writes "We've known for a very long time that nutrition is incredibly important for our bodies and our weight. We now know that it's just as important for looking after our minds. Many foods contain nutrients that directly help improve the function of our brains."[46]

Benefits: A new study finds that people who consume two servings of fruit per day have 36% lower odds of developing Type 2 diabetes than those who consume less than half a serving.[47] Other benefits include weight loss, heart health, strong bones and teeth, better mood and energy levels, and improved memory and brain health.

Top Tips: Invest in a nutritionist such as Libby Linford, a nutritionist and mindful-eating practitioner such as Carrie Smith, a ketogenic naturopath such as Jennifer Harper-Deacon or to a health coach such as Anna Anderson if you find it hard to keep a healthy regime. Anna has helped hundreds of women to smash the destructive cycle of dieting. (Details of all these individuals are on page 210 in *Further Resources*.)

Time-Poor Tips: Plan your meals/diet ahead of time, batch cook, make green juices (and healthy soups) and freeze them. Alternatively, cut up the ingredients ahead of time, place them in a bag or container and freeze them, ready for making into juices/ soups. Purchase a weekly pill container and sort your vitamins into it on a Sunday night when you plan your week, which I explain later in *Chapter 4*.

Budget Friendly Tips: Look up recipes from the Mediterranean diet online. Frozen vegetables and fruit can sometimes be a cheaper option to fresh.

Mighty Motivation Magic Hormones: Inconclusive.

Clothes – You are what you wear

I don't know about you, but my clothes, jewellery and make-up always make me feel so much better (particularly through the various COVID-19 lockdowns), as well as including exercise and dressing well in my self-care routine. How you look on the outside hugely influences how you feel on the inside. It can make you feel more confident and, on a good day and in the right clothes, 10 years younger!

I'm honouring clothes and jewellery under the title of self-care because they made such a difference to my mood during lockdown, and for so many others too. I've also come to realise I have a slight obsession with colourful earrings, but I don't care, because they make me smile. I found one of those earring stands, and at last count, I have 52 pairs of earrings! It might be useful to explain that I only got my ears pierced about two years ago, so the novelty hasn't worn off yet, and if you haven't done it yet, I highly recommend it. Of course, colourful earrings may not be your thing, so I'd encourage you to find an alternative that works for you, such as other types of jewellery, shoes, colourful scarves or painting your nails.

My amazing friend Emma Shoe, from Styling You Well, is a personal stylist and sustainability champion of circular and preloved fashion, and she is on a mission to help women buy fewer clothes and wear each item more often. Emma has been inspiring me to buy less, wear more of my clothes and dress more colourfully since she styled me amazingly well a couple of years ago. We had an incredible wardrobe session where she showed me clothes combinations that I'd never have thought of. She works intuitively with the goal to empathise with, uplift, nurture, inspire, hand hold and gently push women to become the best version of themselves through their style. Plus, she is always thinking about sustainability. It felt like I had a new wardrobe after my 4 hours with her.

There are specific colours that can actually increase the production of serotonin in the brain, which is the mood lifter.

According to David Zyler in his book *Color Your Style: How to Wear Your True Colors*,[48] yellow is the colour of happiness, the sun and laughter. Studies show that the colour yellow increases the production of serotonin in the brain, speeds up metabolism and lifts the mood of all those around it.[49,50] In addition, yellow increases concentration and attention, so it's often used on billboards, advertising sites, road signs and street lines. Shades of yellow in clothing are often worn by active, creative and addictive people. They're bright dreamers and adventurers, who are ready to explore and conquer.[51]

Soft pink is considered to be calm, warm and feminine, and it's one of the most powerful sedatives. In some prisons, the walls are painted in shades of pink to reduce the level of aggression; one scientific study on this identifies that, within a week of doing this, the aggression of the prisoners had dissipated.[52]

Zyler also details in his book that those who love pink are romantic, optimistic and self-righteous (in a good sense).[53] As a rule, they're people who appreciate kindness and comfort above everything else.

Jules Standish, author of *How Not To Wear Black*, says this:[54]

> *As the physiological and psychological effects of color are central to your wellbeing and to the way you present yourself, it is also vital to your health, beauty and self-confidence.*

> *Understanding that the connection between the colors you are most attracted to can also reflect your personal coloring and temperament...*

In another article, she wrote this:[55]

> *Looking at warm, bright colours, such as red or pink, releases dopamine – known as the 'feel-good hormone' – which can improve our mood, heighten the attention span and even boost our sex drive. Cool blues, on the other hand, have been linked to the release of oxytocin, making you feel calm.*

Finally, I wanted to mention a great friend of mine, Karen Hale, an empowerment and public speaking coach. I've had the pleasure of working with Karen numerous times over the past 16 years, as have some of my clients, and I've received her help in various corporate roles with respect to personal brand, presence and communication, as well as public-speaking coaching. She has an incredible gift of making everybody she works with feel completely relaxed, and she's able to bring the best out of a person with ease. She has always been my go-to person whenever I have nerves before presenting at a workshop or event.

Recap: How you look on the outside hugely influences how you feel on the inside.

Facts: Dopamine, oxytocin and serotonin – feel-good hormones that affect our mood and motivation – are all produced by wearing (or seeing) certain different colours and taking care of our appearance on a daily basis.

Benefits: Certain colours can improve your mood, heighten your attention span, boost your sex drive and reduce aggression.

Top Tips: Even if you don't feel like dressing well, just do it. Have a shower, make your bed, slap on some make-up, spray on some perfume and dress in something that makes you feel great, and you can't help but feel better. Enlist a stylist like Emma to help you declutter your wardrobe and show you how to combine clothes or take you shopping, either shopping for preloved or new. You'll feel a million dollars, take my word for it.

Time-Poor Tips: Try putting on a little make-up, jewellery, some perfume and something colourful, and then see how it makes you feel.

Budget Friendly Tips: Charity shops are brilliant for picking up bargains. I try to only shop for clothes in charity shops now. It's better for the planet too!

Mighty Motivation Magic Hormones: Dopamine, oxytocin and serotonin.

> *"Mere colour, unspoiled by meaning, and unallied with definite form, can speak to the soul in a thousand different ways."*
>
> *- Oscar Wilde*

Mobile phones – Love or hate?

Thanks to Instagram, this book was born. I started my Instagram account in February 2018, which coincided with running my vision board workshops, and I've included much of the content within the pages of this book.

I've spent a lot of time reflecting on the damage that smart/ mobile phone usage has on our existence. My view is conflicting; on days where I'm using social media to market my coaching and workshops, and to interact with others, connect and comment, I love it. But on days when my mind monkeys (mental chatter) take over, compare me to everybody else and make me feel like shit, I hate it. And I suspect you may feel the same.

Also, switch-tasking is a recognised thing; it's the process when you're in the middle of something really important, you hear your phone ping and you think, *Ooh exciting, I wonder what or who that is?* so then you pick your phone up, and before you know it, you're scrolling away happily, wasting minutes and focus. Apparently, this habit also increases the production of cortisol (the stress hormone) as well as adrenaline (the flight or fight hormone), which results in an overstimulated brain, meaning you can't think clearly. A great solution for this situation is to place your phone in another room so it isn't a distraction – out of sight, out of mind.

Alternatively, there are apps that can help, such as Moment and RealizD, which can help to reduce your phone usage by tracking how often you open your phone. There are others – Forest and OurPact – which were built with parents in mind. Offtime, Freedom, ShutApp and SPACE have also been developed as personalised behaviour-change apps designed to help users think about how they use their phones and how it affects their lives. I suppose these apps wouldn't exist if it wasn't such a problem, so my advice would be that if you think you have a problem, try one of these apps.

It's worth reading this interesting *Forbes* article, which states "Facebook conjures up a perception of social isolation" (Luckily, I'm not on there too much!); "Social media use is linked to greater feelings of social isolation"; "any kind of comparison (to others) is linked to depressive symptoms"; and "Social media use triggers feelings of jealousy."[56]

Research has shown that taking a rest and a break from social media is good for us.[57] I've taken a few breaks from social media and smart phone usage, up to two months previously, and it has done me a lot of good. I had a house move to plan and action, and with all the chaos that moving entailed, I knew that less mobile phone and social media usage would make for some quality time out to get really organised, get routines back in place, and have some rest time to think about goals and plans for the coming months. It was brilliant.

I remember feeling wonderfully refreshed, restored and raring to go. It was also great to have the time to reflect on my first 6 months of facilitating workshops. I realised during this time that it's okay to rest and it's okay to have time out; in fact, it's so important that I'd urge you to give it a go, even if it's just a few days off social media and using your phone. You'll gain renewed energy, creativity and new ideas, I promise.

At the time of writing, I noticed on Instagram that Dr Rangan Chatterjee has said he is taking a month off social media: "Having a period of time off social media allows me to tune into myself. Having some time away allows us to hear our own voice more clearly. Benefits for me include more calm, mental stillness, and an enhanced ability to be present with the most important people in my life."[58]

Recap: It's never a bad thing to have time away from your mobile phone. In fact, doing this can renew your energy, increase your creativity and give you new ideas. They can be distracting, cause sleep disorders, waste our time and create more stress in our lives. There are many apps that can help, including those that monitor mobile usage (Moment and RealizD), those for parents (Forest and OurPact) and behaviour-change apps (Offtime, Freedom, ShutApp and SPACE).

Facts: A staggering 5 billion people around the world now own a smart/mobile phone. Research says that roughly half of the 3.7 hours that each person spends using a mobile phone each day is using social and communications apps.[59] Mobile phones are impacting our attention spans. A study conducted at Hankamer School of Business, Baylor University, confirms that smartphones can actually impact your relationships quite negatively and make you more depressed as a result of your attention span being wrecked.[60]

Benefits: Smart/mobile phones are convenient, you can shop while on the move, they're great for staying organised, they store photos and information, file sharing is easy, you can bank on them, social media can help your business move forwards and connect you with other people, you always have something to do when waiting for somebody / an appointment, you can track and improve your health and fitness, you can call somebody in an emergency, they tell the time, they are brilliant as a flashlight, and you can stay on top of world events.

Top Tips: Try not to look at your phone first thing in the morning – that means scrolling through social media then – as it'll make you less productive during the day. Limit the time you spend on your phone on a daily basis.

Time-Poor Tips: Put your phone in another room for undisturbed work, or play time with your dog, children or other adults – you'll definitely make up time in your day this way!

Budget Friendly Tips: Community Calling, run by Hubbub, provides free mobile-phone and digital-skills training.

Mighty Motivation Magic Hormones: Dopamine.

"Life is what happens when your cell phone is charging."

– Unknown

The to-do list – Why a list of three things really works

Around 15 years ago, I was working at an amazing company called Ten Group. Imagine a virtual personal assistant (PA) service to high-net-worth, very-important-person (VIP) individuals who had supercharged needs! There were two massive learnings that I took away from working there, which are things that I still do to this day.

The first is in honour of a lovely girl called Joanne Crovini, who was in my team. Each night before she left the office, I'd watch Joanne produce her beautifully written list of things to do the next day, on a whole page, and I was rather in awe of her organisational skills. I soon followed suit, feeling more organised and structured than ever before, and I loved the effect caused by crossing things off that list daily.

The second is from some amazing training we had from a guy called David McClements around the subject of time management and doing the 'monster' (that is, the biggest task and/or the one you're putting off / dreading the most) on your daily to-do list first. David's system was revolutionary, and this was before the book *Eat That Frog* by Brian Tracy came out in 2013, but it's based around the same idea. I think I prefer the monster analogy.

If you aren't used to writing a list the night before and prefer to do it in the morning, studies have shown that people perform better when they've written down what they need to do,[61] so any list writing is essentially good. Sunday evenings are also particularly good for spending 20 minutes planning your week ahead and making yourself accountable to a friend for your list/ goals; more on that in *Chapter 4*.

I write my daily list in my *The 6-Minute Diary* or in one of my many notebooks (I just counted them, and I have 25! Is that too many?); it's a list of no more than three things at a time, and I then number them in order of priority and put the monster first.

Please note, I'm not perfect; I do get sabotaged by my mind monkeys and a bit of lovely procrastination at times, but at least I'm aware of it!

Be as specific as you can about each thing on your list, and be realistic in terms of what's achievable; break up big tasks into chunks (again, more on that in *Chapter 4*), give the time commitment you're going to spend on it, and also think creatively to see if you can get any help with it! There's more on assistance in *Chapter 5*.

A study done by The Draugiem Group says that the formula for perfect productivity is working for 52 minutes and then taking a break for 17 minutes;[62] there are different versions of this, but this one works really well. Set an alarm for this if you can. Or even better, use a timer. I purchased a 60-minute countdown timer at the beginning of 2020, which has been the perfect addition to my desk, and I now use it daily to work more productively. It has a loud alarm to remind me to take a break. I also use it to time the 17 minutes of my break times so I don't overdo them!

Use the 17 minutes of your break to do something nice and rewarding, such as taking a quick walk, chatting with a friend, making a hot drink, reading a book, etc. You're rewarding your brain and producing dopamine, which will motivate you to move towards ticking things off your list and getting more done. There's also the Pomodoro Technique,[63] which is working for 25 minutes and then taking a break for 5; this is also really great for productivity. I tend to use both systems, and they both work really well. I also have the 52/17 method to thank for facilitating my writing of this book.

It's okay to have a longer list of things to do / goals as a brain dump of what you want to achieve that week/month on a separate list (I use a system called Trello, a Google doc or a notebook).

Be realistic in terms of what's achievable (say, if you have a report to write, note down how many pages/words you're going to write that day and by when).

Also, try not to check your emails, phone, etc. before tackling your number-one task! Even better, put your mobile phone in another room!

If you have a niggle or are thinking about something that's causing anxiety or stress (let's call it the monster again), then make sure that it's on your list; the sooner you do it, the sooner it frees you up to do something else. If you're finding you're procrastinating, just do 15 minutes of work, and you may end up carrying on for longer.

If you manage to finish those three things on your list, then give yourself a huge pat on the back and a reward. When you check an item off or put a line through it on your to-do list, you feel successful, which sends a rush of dopamine into your brain and motivates you to do it again.

Finally, you could also try having a list of things you won't do that day, such as not checking email while working on a task, eating lunch at your desk or losing track of time in between tasks.

Recap: Each evening write your list of three things to do the next day, including your monster as the thing for you to do first. You may also write a longer list of things to do that week (Sunday night is good for doing this) or month. Put your mobile phone in another room to avoid distractions and be super productive. Use a digital system such as Trello, Google Docs or Microsoft (MS) Word if it helps you to be more organised.

Facts: Psychologist and author Dr David Cohen states in an interview in *The Guardian* that lists "dampen anxiety about the chaos of life; they give us a structure, a plan that we can stick to; and they are proof of what we've achieved that day, week or month."[64] A study by professors Masicampo and Baumeister from Wake Forest University reveals that, while tasks we haven't done distract us, just making a plan to get them done can free us from this anxiety.[65]

Benefits: Reduces anxiety and produces the feel-good hormone dopamine when a goal has been achieved.

Top Tips: Each evening write your long list, transfer your three things to your daily list and do the monster first before anything else. You'll feel great once you've achieved it. Again, I'll recommend *The 6-Minute Diary* here, which has a section called 'This is how I will make today great', where I list my three things.

Time-Poor Tips: Plan ahead for the week and write your big list on Sunday night in bed before you go to sleep; it won't take long.

Budget Friendly Tips: Charity shops often have low-cost diaries and notepads.

Mighty Motivation Magic Hormones: Dopamine.

"Have the courage to follow your heart and intuition. They somehow already know what you truly want to become."

- Steve Jobs

Sleep – The great healer

In May 2018, I was lucky enough to spend a wonderful week sunning myself on a sun lounger beside a turquoise pool on the beautiful Greek island of Mykonos. I became completely obsessed with the book I was reading. That book has become the most important book that I've ever read.

Why We Sleep by Professor Matthew Walker is, I believe, an essential read for everybody, whatever their age. I've shared some of its findings with anybody willing to listen – friends, family and colleagues – and it makes for an eye-opening and fascinating read.

Professor Walker is the professor of neuroscience and psychology at the University of California, Berkeley; he has been studying sleep for 20 years; and it took 4.5 years to write his book. His research and findings include that we all need to sleep 7–9 hours a day, otherwise our immune system is essentially 'demolished'.[66]

In this book, he demonstrates through his research how sleep (or lack thereof) links to mental health issues, weight gain and many other health problems: "Emerging from this research renaissance is an unequivocal message: sleep is the single most effective thing we can do to reset our brain and body health each day."[67]

This book has completely changed my relationship with sleep. My bed has always had a special place in my heart, but – and don't laugh – I love it even more now, as now I know the benefits of prioritising it and what getting Professor Walker's recommended amount of sleep is doing for so many aspects of my life.

He also advises not drinking caffeine after 1pm (this includes decaffeinated drinks, as decaf still contains small amounts of caffeine), as it stays in your system for eight hours and affects your rapid eye movement (REM) / deep sleep; he also – and I'm really sorry to say this – states that the same effect is true of alcohol. And, no, I'm not perfect all the time. I love a glass of wine or three now and then; that's classed as fun in my book! But I must admit that I now don't drink caffeine after 1pm, swapping it for bought herbal teas or fresh mint tea instead, and it has made a big difference to the quality of my sleep. I've also massively cut down on my alcohol consumption, and I've kept my daily exercise regime going, which helps. If I ever have trouble getting to sleep or I wake up at night, I use either the Calm app (which is the number-one app for meditation and sleep), Insight Timer or a YouTube video (type "sleep meditation" into Google to find a selection).

You'll probably not be surprised to know that the moon, as well as affecting the world's tides, also can have an effect on our sleep. When there's a full moon, it can feel to some like a bit of a disruptive time, which I've discussed with many friends, and we all tend to have similar experiences: more erratic behaviour, tension, tiredness, anxiety or being emotionally upset.

A study has found that people actually sleep 20 minutes less when the moon is full, take 5 minutes longer to fall asleep and experience 30 minutes more of REM sleep, during which most dreaming is believed to occur.[68]

For those who do have trouble sleeping, it's definitely worth investing in working with a sleep specialist. I recommend Motty Varghese, a sleep specialist who uses cognitive behavioural therapy (CBT) to help his clients, with amazing results! CBT is a talking therapy that can help manage sleep issues (and other issues) by changing the way you think and behave. In the meantime, try reducing the amount of caffeine (including decaf) and alcohol you ingest, see what the results are like and try some of the following 'Top Tips'.

Sleep (or nap) pods are becoming more popular. These pods are structures that are often used in corporate or workplace environments where you can go to have a nap. Dr Sarah McKay believes so much in a 20-minute nap during the day that she did a TED talk, 'Indulge your neurobiology', on it, which I highly recommend watching and trying out (see page 213 in *Further Resources* for details).

Recap: It is recommended that you get 7–9 hours of sleep a day. Drinking caffeine after 1pm will affect your sleep; remember, decaf still contains caffeine. Alcohol is a sedative that blocks your REM dream sleep, which is an important part of the sleep cycle.

Facts: Neglecting sleep reduces your creativity, problem-solving ability, decision-making ability, learning, memory, heart health, brain health, mental health, emotional well-being, immune system and even your life span. Dr Matthew Walker writes in his book that sleep produces complex neurochemical baths that improve our brains in various ways; it "restocks the armory of our immune system, helping prevent infection, and warding off all manner of sickness."[69]

Benefits: Not only does sleep 'cleanse' the brain but also everything always seems so much better the next day, as it can give you a new perspective, and potentially, a new way of looking at a challenge, issue, goal or opportunity. Expect to receive a mood boost, a sharper brain, a healthier heart, better immunity and improved weight control as a result.

Top Tips: Having a hot herbal drink before bed, taking a shower or a hot bath with a sprinkling of magnesium salts, and switching off from mobiles, TV and electronic devices an hour before bed all help. Blackout blinds are good, as are eye masks, and if I ever have trouble getting to sleep, I use a great breathing technique that works: breathe in for a count of seven, then breathe out for a count of 11, and keep on repeating this. I also highly recommend Professor Walker's TED talk 'Sleep is your superpower'. Make sure your bedroom is clutter free. If you have a sleep issue, seek professional help; don't just suffer. (I recommend Motty Varghese, who's mentioned in *Further Resources* on page 210; a sleep therapist; or get a local recommendation.)

Time-Poor Tips: See the 'Top Tips' given, which will make falling sleep easier and quicker.

Budget Friendly Tips: Use an app if you're having trouble sleeping, and try any of the 'Top Tips' given.

Mighty Motivation Magic Hormones: Melatonin.

> *"Sleep is the golden chain that binds health and our bodies together."*
>
> – Thomas Dekker

Emotional freedom technique (EFT) – How to reduce stress and anxiety fast

If you knew there was a tool that could help you reduce your stress, anxiety and overwhelm levels in under 10 minutes, how would that make you feel? Especially knowing how the COVID-19 pandemic has affected each and every one of us.

Thankfully, I was introduced to this 10-year-old revolutionary tool in the last year by a wonderful friend and well-being practitioner, Aga Kehinde, who has worked in medicine for 20 years and helps her clients alleviate their stress and anxiety levels using EFT, plus much more.

EFT works by tapping (with your fingers) specific acupressure points (also called meridian points) on the body, primarily on the head and the face, in a particular sequence, starting with the side of the hand, then moving to the face, collarbone, armpit and the top of the head. This is then repeated three times while focusing on the particular issue that's causing the stress.

It's an evidence-based technique and alternative protocol that works to reduce the effects of stress, anxiety, anger, fear and overwhelm. It also works well to diminish limiting beliefs, low-frequency emotion, phobias and post-traumatic stress disorder (PTSD).

Success rates are high. According to EFT founder, Gary Craig, tapping can bring complete or partial relief in about 80% of cases, and the relief is often permanent. Working with a certified EFT practitioner increases the success rate to an impressive 95%.[70]

I've practised EFT during the pandemic, and it's given me amazing benefits, including reducing my stress levels over the space of 10 minutes from a level 8 out of 10 (stress level) down to a 4 out of 10. It's incredible, and I wish that more people would learn about it and use it.

If you find yourself in a distressed state, you can use the following basic technique and also refer to *The EFT Mini-Manual*[71] for a more detailed description:

» **Step 1:** Start by focusing on the negative emotion: your fear, anxiety, worry, sadness or whatever is bothering you. Rate this distress or discomfort on a scale of 0 to 10 (0 being no distress and 10 being extreme distress).

» **Step 2:** In order to maintain your mental focus and keep in the present moment, you need to create a statement – essentially, you'll capture your problem in this statement. This statement should be in the form: "Even though I'm... [insert your problem / feeling], I accept how I feel."

» **Step 3:** Repeat this statement three times while gently tapping on the side of your hand below your little finger (tap with the fingers of your opposite hand). Continue tapping for as long as it takes you to repeat the statement.

» **Step 4:** Tap eight times on each of the eight points on your body (please refer to *The EFT Mini-Manual* for a more detailed explanation and images[72]), while repeating a short reminder phrase to make sure your mind is engaged. The reminder phrase is a shorter version of your initial statement, focusing only on the feeling; for example, "Stressed," "Anxious," or, "Worried."

» **Step 5:** Finally, take a deep breath and rerate your discomfort score.

Tapping on these meridian points while concentrating on accepting and resolving the negative emotion allows us to restore ourselves quickly to a balanced state. We're mindfully acknowledging the state we're in. We use tapping and breathing with compassionate acceptance and positive affirmations, which immediately calms us down.

Tapping is simple, painless and empowering. It can be learnt by anyone, and you can apply it to yourself, whenever you want and wherever you are. Most importantly, tapping gives you the power to manage your own stress and anxiety in a matter of minutes, and its lasting effects will restore control for the moment and the future. Aga Kehinde uses this technique with both her clients and her children (of which she has two) with great success. It's a great technique to use just before putting your children to bed, as it's guaranteed to calm them down. My friend Emma's children also love it.

Recap: EFT is a tool that can help you reduce your stress, anxiety and overwhelm levels in under 10 minutes. It's also used to reduce the effects of anger and fear, diminish limiting beliefs and low-frequency emotion, and to treat phobias and PTSD.

Facts: While writing this book and researching studies on the benefits of EFT, I discovered a pilot study that produced very positive findings:[73] a single 20-minute online group treatment was effective in reducing stress, anxiety and burnout in nurses working with COVID-19 patients during the pandemic.

Benefits: It's so simple that you can learn to do tapping in a few minutes. You don't need to lie down or close your eyes, and once you've got the hang of it, there's no need to listen to a script.

Tapping can be done anywhere or anytime you feel stressed or anxious: at your desk, in your car or even during a quick bathroom break. The improvement is often rapid. Even persistent problems can sometimes be cleared in just a few tapping sessions. Treatment time frames range from one session for phobias to six sessions for PTSD.

Top Tips: Use tapping whenever you notice you're having an anxious or stressful moment; be aware of how you're feeling, step away from whatever you're doing (perhaps sit down), and if you already know a script, then go through the tapping with that script. If you don't have a script, type into Google "EFT tapping"; type either "Aga Kehinde EFT", "Brad Yates EFT" or "Gary Craig EFT" for a demonstration; or contact Aga directly (see page 210 in *Further Resources* for details).

Time-Poor Tips: The great thing about EFT/tapping is that results can be seen in just 10 minutes of tapping. Let me know how you get on.

Budget Friendly Tips: Use the instructions given in this section or those in one of the online videos.

Mighty Motivation Magic Hormones: Produces dopamine and reduces cortisol.

"Your emotional health, your success in the world, and your level of joy can all be dramatically enhanced by shifting the energies that regulate them."

- David Feinstein, PhD

Conclusion

So how did you get on? I've shared a lot of information in this chapter, but if you manage just three of these things daily – let's say affirmations, exercise and gratitude (and, of course, drinking water goes without saying!) – the mighty motivation magic hormones should start kicking in, and you won't be able to help having a mood boost and feeling more positive and motivated. Even better, enlist a friend to do it with and check in with them daily (WhatsApp is useful for this).

Hopefully, you're now beginning to see how important self-care is, and that it's a fundamental pillar to keeping your mind and body strong and healthy.

Key points:

» Toxic positivity is a thing. Make sure you talk about how you're feeling to friends and loved ones, or alternatively, a professional (a counsellor, therapist, etc.); remember that there's no shame or guilt in not being okay. Share this concept with others and see what they think.

» By staying hydrated throughout the day, you'll remain energised and focused, and your concentration will be improved. Your pee should be a light-straw colour. Drink a couple of glasses of water first thing in the morning.

» Affirmations focus your attention on goals, reprogram your subconscious mind and are used to help you create the positive reality you want.

» Exercise is like medicine: it can improve memory and brain function, safeguard against various chronic diseases, facilitate weight management, increase the quality of your sleep, lessen feelings of anxiety and depression, and other things besides.

» Gratitude creates positive emotions such as joy, love and contentment; it turns our mental focus to the positive; and it reduces stress. It's not possible to be both grateful and angry (or fearful or stressed) at once.

» Getting a good night's sleep (7–9 hours) can give you a fresh perspective, and it may also give you a new way of looking at a challenge, issue, goal or opportunity. It can boost your mood, sharpen your brain, make your heart healthier, improve your immunity and give you better control over your weight.

"The way we experience the world around us is a direct reflection of the world within us."

– Gabrielle Bernstein

CHAPTER TWO

STEP 2: ENVIRONMENT

The word 'environment' means so many different things to different people, but the Cambridge Dictionary definition explains it as "the air, water, and land in or on which people, animals, and plants live" and "the conditions that you live or work in and the way that they influence how you feel or how effectively you can work".[74]

Our environment – which includes our friends, family, colleagues, home, habits and lifestyle – impacts us more than we realise. If we alter elements of our environment, it can help us grow and develop.

According to an article by The Royal Australian College of General Practitioners, our physical environment significantly influences our behaviours, cognition, emotions and relationships with others, and it can also have a cumulative effect on our brains.[75]

For the purposes of this book, and to explain my process and the changes I've made to my environment that may help you too, our focus will be on five main areas:

1. Clutter-free living

2. People – friends, family, colleagues and networks

3.   Plants and flowers

4.   Aromatherapy

5.   Music

Clutter-free living

At the time of writing these words, I'm sitting in a co-working space, delighted to have finally left the confines of my COVID-19 working-from-home life. For those lucky enough to live in a large house with multiple rooms to escape to, you'll know how important your environment is to your productivity and working day: the more space you have and the less cluttered the environment, the more room you have for thoughts and a stress-free life.

Our environment influences our behaviour, sleep, happiness and mental health, as well as our motivation to act. It can impact our hormones as well as our mood. Our brains like order. They don't like to be disorganised or surrounded by clutter. Clutter can cause our bodies to release cortisol, the stress hormone associated with a fight-or-flight response. Long-term exposure to clutter can also induce chronic stress, and it can affect our anxiety levels, sleep and ability to focus.[76]

Thanks to Marie Kondo, the Japanese expert in decluttering, we now have a book to refer to – *The Life-Changing Magic of Tidying: A simple, effective way to banish clutter forever* – which, admittedly, I haven't read yet, but I know many whose lives she has transformed, as well as organising their knicker drawer into a beautiful, colourful work of art!

You may also be a fan of the Netflix show *Tidying Up*, which features Marie. Interestingly, she now has another book based around organising your professional life, *Joy at Work,* which has been co-written with Scott Sonenshein, the Henry Gardiner Symonds Professor of Management at Rice University and bestselling author of *Stretch: Unlock the Power of Less – And Achieve More Than You Ever Imagined*; this just goes to show how being less cluttered and more organised is so on trend.

When I look back at my own personal journey, which began with self-care (as described in the previous chapter), a massive declutter most definitely came next, helped along by moving from a house to a one-bedroom flat. In order to sell that house, a massive declutter was needed. It wasn't terrible in terms of clutter because the rooms were large, but the garden needed clearing, weeding and decluttering, and the house needed to be put back in some order so as to sell it more easily.

There's something so cathartic about having a good sort out and declutter, and it will leave you with a real sense of achievement and renewed clarity.

Have you ever noticed how it makes you feel when you have a messy area of your house or your desk? Potentially, quite chaotic, disorganised and fuzzy-headed. You probably recognise that you can't seem to get things done quickly and finished, or you're just super slow.

Sabine Kastner, a professor of neuroscience and psychology at Princeton University, started researching the science of attention in 2008. In an article in *National Geographic*, Kastner explains "Many of us aren't good at processing clutter" and "It can become overwhelming and make our brains do more work to complete simple tasks."[77] The more conflicting stimuli we're dealing with, the more our brain has to work to filter out what we need.

Kastner also finds that people who clean up their homes or workspaces are able to focus better, and their productivity increases: "Other research teams have confirmed that decreasing visual distractions can reduce cognitive load and free up working memory."[78]

Disorganised and messy environments led participants in one study to eat more snacks; they ate twice as many cookies as participants in an organised kitchen environment.[79] Other research shows that being in a messy room will make you twice as likely to eat a chocolate bar than an apple.[80]

If decluttering seems like an overwhelming task, enlist help from family members or friends, and tackle it in 15-minute increments, which is totally doable. You'll find that once you've got started, it gets slightly addictive! Unwanted items can be donated to charity shops, or sold on Gumtree, Facebook Marketplace, eBay, local community sites or Freecycle. And don't forget to declutter your handbag, your pockets, the desktop of your laptop/computer and unnecessary emails.

Finally, the following is a really useful exercise to do to see how your environment is affecting you.

Think about the five places you spend the most time, not including your bed (this could be your sofa, kitchen, desk, workplace, garden, bedroom, etc.):

- » How do you feel when you're in that particular place, room, etc.?

- » Does the feeling change when you leave that place, room, etc.?

Do you feel motivated and love your environment, or do you feel drained? If you feel drained, then have a think about these things:

- » Why do you feel drained?

- » What do you think could be causing this feeling? Is there something specific about the place that makes you feel drained?

- » When did this feeling begin? Can you pinpoint a particular time?

- » What is it exactly about the place that makes you feel drained?

Once you've considered these things, do the following:

- ✓ Imagine how you want to feel about this place instead. Write down (in your notebook) the things that you could change and improve to make it a much better place to spend time.

- ✓ Put a plan in place to make some changes (there will be more on planning in *Chapter 4*).

Recap: Our environment influences our behaviour, sleep, happiness and mental health, as well as our motivation to act. This can influence our hormones as well as our mood. Our brains prefer order, and they don't perform as well in an environment that's disorganised or if we are surrounded by clutter.

Facts: Being exposed to clutter in the long term may cause chronic stress and also impact our anxiety levels, sleep and ability to focus. Clutter acts as a distraction, increasing cognitive overload, and it can reduce our working memory too. Those with extremely cluttered homes are 77% more likely to be overweight.[81]

Benefits: The scientific benefits of clearing clutter include improved sleep, reduced anxiety, better productivity, eating less junk food, more creativity and a clear mind! On the other hand, those who thrive in cluttered environments see an increase in creativity.

Top Tips: If decluttering seems like an overwhelming task, enlist the help of a friend or family member, or even better, an expert declutterer (see page 210 in *Further Resources* for my suggestions)! If you're tackling your decluttering alone, set a timer for 15 minutes and see how you go. Think of the five places you spend the most time in and how they could potentially be affecting your life.

Time-Poor Tips: Throw away, donate or return one item every day for 30 days and see how you feel. Enlist friends or family to help you declutter.

Budget Friendly Tips: You can sell any unwanted items on Facebook Marketplace, eBay, Gumtree or your local Nextdoor.

Mighty Motivation Magic Hormones: Reduces the stress hormone, cortisol.

"Out of clutter, find simplicity. From discord, find harmony. In the middle of difficulty lies opportunity."

– Albert Einstein

People – Friends, family, colleagues and networks

An article by Dr Sarah McKay concludes that having strong social connections in our lives helps promote brain health, decreases rates of heart disease, produces a stronger immune system, lowers blood pressure and reduces rates of dementia.[82] Friends and family can help us deal with stress, make better lifestyle choices that keep us strong, and allow us to rebound from health issues and disease more quickly. Incredible!

I feel very lucky and honoured to have the amazing family and group of friends that exist in my life, and the same goes for my clients, colleagues and networks. I can safely say that I do surround myself with people who are supportive, kind, generous and wise, and who have always been there for me throughout the roller coaster of life. I hope very much that some, if not all, of this also exists in your life.

"You are the average of the five people you spend the most time with," says entrepreneur and motivational speaker Jim Rohn. With this in mind, we should think about those whom we spend time with in the same way we think about what we eat and how we're exercising. Do they inspire you? What do they add to your life? Are they positive? Do they encourage you and support your dreams? If the answer to these questions is yes, then they can add lots of value to your life and improve your chances for success.

I know only too well what it's like to be in an environment with negative people who disagree with dreaming, are unsupportive and aren't adding the right value. My advice would be to try to remove these individuals from your life. This may sound harsh, but they'll only hold you back.

Close relationships, more than money or fame, are what keep people happy throughout their lives, explains an article detailing Harvard University's 80-year study of adult development.[83] It proves that embracing community helps us live longer and be happier.

The same goes with your colleagues. According to the Gallup organisation, people who have a best friend at work are seven times more likely to be engaged in their jobs.[84] However, it doesn't have to be a best friend forever (BFF). Gallup also identifies that people who simply have a good friend in the workplace are more likely to be happy. What's more, good work relationships are linked to better customer engagement and increased profit.

Humans are naturally social beings, and considering we spend one-third of our lives working, it's going to make it easier and more enjoyable to have good relationships with our colleagues. The more comfortable co-workers are with each other, the more confident they feel voicing opinions, brainstorming and going along with new ideas. Teamwork is essential for embracing change, creating and innovating. When people see the successes from working together in this way, group morale and productivity soars.

Good work relationships give you freedom. Instead of spending time and energy dealing with negative relationships, you can instead focus on opportunities such as winning business or personal development.

Being part of a network or group can also provide much value and connection, particularly if you are a small-business owner working mainly on your own. I talk about networks and networking in more detail in *Chapter 5*, but active networking is vital to career or business growth. Often confused with selling, networking is about building long-term relationships and a good reputation over time. It involves meeting and getting to know people whom you can assist and who can potentially help you in return. Your network includes everyone from your friends and family to work colleagues and members of groups you belong to. Although I'm not a natural networker, I've had oodles of experience over the years, and I've come to realise how important it is as a small-business owner. The benefits also include strengthened relationships; fresh ideas; a raised profile; access to opportunities, information, advice and support; and, more crucially, connection with others.

Similar to the earlier exercise, another useful exercise to do is to see how people in your life affect you.

Think about the five people you spend the most time with:

- »   How do you feel when you're in the presence of each of these people?

- »   Do you feel uplifted, motivated or drained?

- »   Does the feeling change when they leave you or you leave them?

- »   Be specific; is it their energy or the things that they say that cause the feeling?

- »   When did these feelings begin? Can you pinpoint a time?

- »   What do you think you need to change? Do you need to talk to them or just not see them often/again? Are they adding positive value to your life?

Perhaps you could spend a bit of time thinking about this regarding other friends in your life also.

Finally, a research project called 'Blue Zones' has identified places in the world where more people reach the age of 100 than anywhere else in the world.[85] The five most well-known Blue Zones are in areas of Greece, Japan, Sardinia, California and Costa Rica. Blue Zone residents share specific characteristics: they all move naturally (taking regular, moderate physical activity), they have purpose in their lives, they have little stress, they are semi-vegetarians, they engage in family life, they are spiritual/religious, they have a moderate alcohol intake, and they live in a community where people of all ages are socially active and integrated into their communities. We can take the lesson from these residents that living a slower, simpler, healthier and more connected life can make us much happier.

Recap: Human connection is a basic need that our lives benefit from, and it's to our detriment if we are lacking in this.

Facts: In a study mentioned in a HuffPost article, 70% of employees say having friends at work is the most crucial element in maintaining a happy working life, and 58% of men would refuse a higher-paying job if it meant not getting along with their co-workers.[86]

Benefits: Having social connections can lower anxiety and depression, helps us regulate our emotions, leads to higher self-esteem and empathy, and actually improves our immune systems. By neglecting our need to connect, we put our health at risk.

Top Tips: Surround yourself with positive people who lift you up, inspire you, believe in you and allow you to dream, with no judgement.

Time-Poor Tip: Send a quick text or message to friends, family, colleagues and/or clients when they pop into your head. Everybody loves a little message to say you're thinking of them.

Budget Friendly Tips: It costs nothing to review friendships and connections, or invest more time in developing good relationships with your family, friends, colleagues and networks who make you feel great, lift you up, support and encourage you.

Mighty Motivation Magic Hormones: Dopamine.

*"Surround yourself with beautiful and positive people,
who love you and believe in you."*

- Bryant McGill

Plants and flowers

According to research, plants can have a really positive impact on your working day.[87] Furthermore, flowers and ornamental plants increase levels of positive energy and help people feel secure and relaxed.

In 2014, a team of psychologists from Exeter University published the results of a study into the impact of plants in offices.[88] They found that adding even a few indoor plants to the workspace enabled employees to become 15% more productive. The benefits are clear: employees felt better, and as a result, their performance in memory retention and other basic tests improved substantially. *A Manchester Evening News* post from August 2019 reveals that GPs in Manchester have actually started to prescribe pot plants (mainly herbs) to patients![89] "'What was important,' said team leader Dr Chris Knight, 'was that everybody could see a plant from their desk. If you're working in an environment where there's something to get you psychologically engaged, you're happier and you work better.'"

According to NASA research, plants absorb volatile organic compounds and move them down to their roots, where microbes get to work and break them down.[90] Over a 24-hour period, indoor plants can remove up to 87% of air toxins.

Flowers do more than just brighten your room: they can have an uplifting and revitalising effect on your mood too. But more than just providing a hit of happiness, research has shown that the impact can last for days,[91] so it's way more powerful than that bar of chocolate and significantly fewer calories! Flowers can also chase away anxieties, worries and the blues, making people feel less depressed, troubled or agitated. They can induce a more positive outlook on life, boosting energy and happiness. Even the smell can help relieve anxiety, and they are the ideal antidote to stress.

Studies have shown that just looking at a picture of the natural world can reduce stress and provide other well-being benefits.[92]

The brilliant book *Losing Eden: Why our minds need the wild* by journalist Lucy Jones explores how and why connecting with the living world can so drastically affect our health.[93] Her advice is to get out in nature; it's a cheap and easy way to get an instant mood boost.

The wonderful world of biophilia (meaning a love of nature) focuses on humans' innate attraction to nature and natural processes. Biophilic design is of ever-increasing importance to our health and well-being in the built environment. Statistics show you can learn 20–26% more if you learn in a biophilic space designed with plants and nature in mind.[94]

Finally, if you love gardening, Lucy mentions in her book that there's an antidepressant effect from getting soil on the skin; a species of bacteria in the soil called *Mycobacterium vaccae* stimulates the brain to create more serotonin, the happy chemical. So, spending more time in the dirt and watching the magic of plants growing is good for you. No wonder people love gardening so much!

For those of you who may live in a flat and have no outside space, windowsills (inside and outside) are great places for growing plants, particularly herbs, or use a plant hanger or spaces on shelves dotted around. Allotments have become more popular in the last few years, you could see what your local community's doing in terms of rewilding in your area or community growing, or you could look up your local 'forest bathing' event (see 'Forest bathing' section on page 180 for details).

Recap: Growing plants in your environment can improve your productivity by 15%. Having both flowers and plants in your environment can have a really positive impact on your well-being, as does gardening.

Facts: Research conducted by the American Society for Horticultural Science reveals that fresh flowers actually have the capacity to ease physical pain and feelings of anxiety.[95] Indoor plants offer two potential benefits for us: improved psychological (mental) well-being and improved physical human health (i.e. they support fitness and general health).

Benefits: The psychological benefits of indoor plants are an improved mood, reduced stress levels, increased worker productivity (from adding plants to office environments in particular), increased reaction speed in a computer-based task, improved attention span (this is identified in some scientific studies, but not all) and increased pain tolerance (for example, where plants were used in hospital settings).

The physical health benefits of indoor plants are reduced blood pressure, reduced fatigue and headaches reduced by 20–25%,[96,97] and patients in hospital rooms with plants have reported decreased post-operative pain.[98]

Top Tips: The Kentia palm or *Howea forsteriana*, a striking plant, is a brilliant all-rounder that has a big impact on any room in your home, and it's easy to keep – even those with green-fingers issues will be pleasantly surprised at how simple they are to tend to. Even I have managed to keep one alive for a few years! Buy your flowers at the local market/florist, as it's good to support local businesses when you can. I highly recommend Kate Avery Flowers for beautiful flower arrangements for weddings, for bespoke floristry tuition and for wedding flowers, as well as Hannah Martin Flowers (see page 210 in *Further Resources* for details).

Time-Poor Tips: A fake plant or flowers is better than no plant or flowers at all. They are easier to manage, and there are some cheap options online, or I recommend Emily Jane Little at Faux Bloom Designs for beautiful, unique, sustainable faux-flower arrangements (see page 210 in *Further Resources* for details).

Budget Friendly Tips: Supermarkets sometimes get rid of out-of-date or older plants and flowers, or you could ask stallholders at your local market at the end of the day – they'll usually sell flowers half price. Kate Avery Flowers recommends charity shops as being good places to find fake plants or flowers.

Mighty Motivation Magic Hormones: Serotonin, dopamine and oxytocin.

"A flower does not use words to announce its arrival to the world; it just blooms."

– Matshona Dhliwayo

Aromatherapy

My friend Belle Brocks, of Annabel Brocks clothing company, cemented my interest in aromatherapy. Over the years, Belle has shared her amazing knowledge with me, and I've read up on which oils are good for what and their different benefits.

When I run my workshops in difference spaces, a diffuser with aromatherapy oils for the room forms the basis of the start of the day, usually using different citrus oils, which helps with clarity. At home I also burn aromatherapy candles and use my diffuser with different oils because of the many well-being benefits.

Aromatherapy, or essential-oil therapy, refers to a range of traditional, alternative and complementary therapies that use essential oils and other aromatic plant compounds. Amazingly, it is believed that essential oils have been used for nearly 6,000 years, with the aim of improving a person's health or mood.

Several lab studies have confirmed that diffusing essential oils such as lavender is shown to reduce stress and help relieve anxiety in medical patients.[99] Preliminary studies have also identified that oil diffusers can help alleviate symptoms of depression when combined with massage.[100]

Belle loves her essential oils so much that she created an amazing business using them: Hawkins Organic produces natural grooming products for humans, hounds and horses. I buy her amazing dog shampoos, which I now use for my hair. They're good enough for my dog, and good enough for me!

Belle has survived two cancer journeys, and she started to use aromatherapy oils when she was going through chemotherapy; since then, they've become very much part of her daily life, as she feels they've helped her through a number of challenging situations and life's roller coaster.

Unlike candles or air fresheners, oil diffusers release cleansing molecules into the air, which work to purify it, not overload it with unhealthy chemicals. Electronic diffusers also don't pose the fire risk that candles do. Plus, they contain the added feature of interchangeability, which means you can change oil types for different scents and health benefits. Belle's advice is that if you're thinking of buying a diffuser, the Tisserand one is a good starting point, and if you want to blow the budget, you can have a gorgeous, ceramic-looking, designer one from Neom.

It's worth spending a little extra on organically certified oils that are vegan friendly and cruelty free; knowing the source of your oils means you'll be getting much better quality. Good places to start looking for oils are Neals Yard, Tisserand, dōTERRA and Neom. They all offer premixed blends, which are quick and easy to use. Tisserand offers a clever rollerball applicator, so you can carry the oils around with you; focus, relax and de-stress oils are all good. It also has a well-being pack, which is a lovely gift for yourself or a friend.

Do make sure you carry out your own research, as some oils are toxic to animals (see 'Top Tips' section on page 107 for details), particularly dogs and cats, or for pregnant women or people with allergies.

Here are some of the main oils and what they're good for:

- ✓ Lime – Focus and an energy boost
- ✓ Grapefruit – A stress buster and reduces mental fatigue
- ✓ Lemongrass – Uplifting, invigorating and can help clear the mind

- ✓ Geranium – Helps lessen feelings of stress and calms nerves
- ✓ Chamomile – Helps reduce anxiety, boost your mood and eliminate stress
- ✓ Lavender – Helps you fall asleep and improves the overall quality of rest; it may also help with reducing pain and improving the quality of life for people with dementia

Recap: Essential oils have been used for around 6,000 years, often for their therapeutic and medicinal benefits, to enhance a person's health or mood.

Facts: Essential oils are highly concentrated versions of the natural oils found in plants. These oils are extracted from the plants by the process of distillation, which is done using water or steam. The oils are obtained from the bark, flowers, stems, leaves and roots of the plant. The product of the distillation is a highly concentrated plant extract, an essential oil, which has the healing properties and fragrance of the plant it was taken from.

Benefits: Some studies have determined that aromatherapy has health benefits, including relief from pain, anxiety and depression; improved quality of life, particularly for people with chronic health conditions; and improved sleep.[101] The Arthritis Foundation states that aromatherapy with lavender oil may help with reducing pain for people with osteoarthritis of the knee, improve quality of life for people with dementia, and reduce pain for people with kidney stones.[102]

Top Tips: It's important to be aware of which oils are toxic to dogs or other animals; these include cinnamon, citrus, pennyroyal, peppermint, pine, sweet birch, tea tree (melaleuca), wintergreen and ylang ylang. If you're considering aromatherapy, consult your doctor and a trained aromatherapist about the possible risks and benefits, or speak to somebody such as Dawn Lovejoy (see page 210 in *Further Resources* for details) at dōTERRA to get advice on which oils are best for what.

Time-Poor Tips: Once a diffuser has been set up with water and oils, it can be turned on just with a flick of a switch. Or you could put a few drops of your chosen essential oil in your bath.

Budget Friendly Tips: Put a message on Facebook Marketplace to see if anybody is getting rid of a diffuser and oils that was an unwanted gift, or ask around in your local community.

Mighty Motivation Magic Hormones: Reduces the stress hormone, cortisol.

"Smell is a potent wizard that transports you across thousands of miles and all the years you have lived."

- Helen Keller

Music

I try not to take music for granted. Listening to it has so many benefits, including relieving anxiety, increasing motivation, potentially improving sleep and possibly enhancing performance. I use meditation music in my physical workshops to improve concentration and clarity. I even put together a Spotify playlist called 'The Motivation Clinic Mood Boosters', which I've listened to while writing parts of this book, and it has kept me motivated.

Some mornings, on my run, I switch from podcasts or silence to music, and I'm so glad I do. Constantly wanting to learn or listening to another inspiring person is fabulous, but sometimes music is what you need!

The benefits are plentiful, including the following:

* Running faster!

* Motivation

* Energy

* Inspiration

* Fire in your belly

* Excitement

Listening to instrumental music, especially music that gives you shivers down your spine, can increase dopamine production in your brain. Simply listening to any music you enjoy may help put you in a good mood. This positive change in your mood can also increase serotonin production. Imagine the energy and motivation you'll get from listening to music plus running – a dopamine and serotonin overload. With this, you can't help but feel great!

Recap: Just 5 minutes of blasting out a track you love (and dancing to it too) can really shift your mood. If you haven't done this for a while, here's your reminder. Go and enjoy getting lost in a bit of music, and turn it up!

Facts: Research has proved that when you listen to music you like, your brain releases dopamine, a feel-good neurotransmitter.[103] In this study, Valorie Salimpoor, a neuroscientist at McGill University, got eight music-lovers to listen to their favourite music, and then she injected them with a radioactive substance that binds to dopamine receptors. A positron emission tomography (PET) scan showed that large amounts of dopamine were released, which biologically caused the participants to feel emotions such as happiness, excitement and joy.

Marcelo Bigliassi and his colleagues found that runners who listen to fast or slow motivational music completed the first 800 metres of their run faster than runners who listened to calm music or ran without music.[104] If you want to take your running up a notch, listen to songs that inspire you. My great friend Carolyn can only run if she is listening to music.

Another study has shown that, generally, 10%–30% of people worldwide suffer from insomnia, but that can be up to 60% in some places.[105] The same study indicates it's common in older adults, females and those with ill health (medical or mental). A study has determined that students who listen to relaxing classical music for 45 minutes before getting into bed sleep significantly better than students who listened to an audiobook or did nothing different from their normal routine.[106]

A study by Hans Joachim Trappe in Germany also demonstrates that music can benefit patients with depressive symptoms, depending on the type of music.[107] Meditative sounds and classical music lifted people up, but techno and heavy metal brought people down even more.

Benefits: Plato had it right when he said, "Music and rhythm find their way into the secret places of the soul." No matter whether you're young or old, healthy or sick, happy or sad, music can improve the quality of your life in numerous ways. Music makes you happier, enhances your running performance, lowers the amount of the stress hormone (cortisol) in your body, improves your health, boosts your immune system, helps you sleep better, reduces depression, helps you eat less, strengthens learning and memory, relaxes patients before and after surgery, reduces pain, helps Alzheimer's patients remember, improves recovery in stroke patients, and increases verbal intelligence and academic performance.

Top Tips: The next time you feel low, put on some classical or meditative music to lift your spirits, or listen to your favourite songs. Try a different music style or genre to what you usually prefer, listen to a whole album or give an analogue record player a go.

Time-Poor Tip: Play some music loud in the car, swap the radio for your favourite playlist and have a dance round the kitchen while cooking or waiting for the kettle to boil, or play music when you're out walking or exercising.

Budget Friendly Tips: Listen to the radio or free music online.

Mighty Motivation Magic Hormones: Oxytocin and dopamine.

"Music is the true breath of life. We eat so we won't starve to death. We sing so we can hear ourselves live."

- Yasmina Khadra

Conclusion

We've now come to the end of *Chapter 2*. As a reminder, our individual environment – our own friends, family, colleagues, home, habits and lifestyle – impacts us so much more than we realise. We can grow and develop when we alter elements of our environment.

So how did you get on? Perhaps you realised that you live in a wonderfully clutter-free world, that you could do with adding a few green friends (plants) to your home or work environment, or that you would benefit from including some more music to your world.

Key points:

» There are many scientific benefits of a good decluttering, which include better sleep, less anxiety, more productivity, eating less junk food, greater creativity and a clear mind! Our brains don't do well with being disorganised or surrounded by clutter.

» It's good to surround yourself with people who are positive and will lift you up. When we have good social connections it can reduce anxiety and depression, aid us in controlling our emotions, engender higher self-esteem and empathy, and even bolster our immune systems.

» Fresh flowers have the capacity to ease physical pain and feelings of anxiety, and plants can have a really positive impact on your working day.

» Aromatherapy can help reduce pain, anxiety and depression; increase quality of life, particularly for people with chronic health conditions; and enhance sleep.

» Music has so many benefits, including making you happier, improving running performance, reducing the amount of cortisol (the stress hormone) in your body, making you healthier, supporting your immune system, facilitating improved sleep, lessening depression, aiding you to eat less, and boosting learning and memory.

CHAPTER THREE

STEP 3: YOUR WHY

Our purpose is why we exist. Our values define how we behave. There will be more on values later, but let's first talk about our why and its importance in life.

I realised in 2017 that understanding my why, my purpose in life, was the single most important thing I could do to kick-start my path towards being a better, happier and more fulfilled me. During my varied career and life, I hadn't thought seriously about this question or dug deep to really think about why I was taking a particular path. I made many changes and tried working in different industries, but this question of "Why?" was never at the front of my mind, and it had never occurred to me before to ask myself this. A coach or mentor would have been a useful addition to my scattergun approach! Let me take you through the process that I now know really works, and it's the one I also take my clients through when they aren't clear on what path to take next and are floundering, stuck, feeling lost and without purpose in life.

Finding your why

When was the last time you stopped and thought, *Why? Why am I doing what I'm doing? What's the purpose of what I'm doing? Do I need to be doing this? Do I enjoy doing this? Should somebody else be doing this? Could I outsource this? Do my values align with what I'm doing right now? Am I happy? Does what I do on a day-to-day basis make me feel good?*

In 5 years' time, if you look back on your life right now, would you be proud and excited with what you're doing? Is it meaningful, does it bring you joy, and are you happy and fulfilled? If the answers to these questions stop you in your tracks, then perhaps you have a little bit of self-enlightening work to do.

Purpose

It took me 48 years to find my true purpose, but that's only because I didn't know where to look and because it wasn't taught at school. Purpose need not be a massive mission. You don't need to be the next Ruth Bader Ginsburg, J.K. Rowling or Oprah, nor should you ever think that you're playing too small.

Yes, some of us do have big purposes, and I always encourage others to dream big and keep seeing the brightest, most exciting future ahead of you (more on that later). Some of us are fulfilled by our own personal dream, and that's great! Be it taking care of children, being a support person in the background, taking care of a building or a property, or being in the same job that you love for years. All are just as valuable, just as worthwhile and just as meaningful, ultimately, we all have a different personal map of the world, and that's what makes our existence on this planet all the more interesting, in my opinion.

It's a matter of what's right for you on a deeper level. Each option is still needed in the world in some way. Each of us is unique, with very unique gifts. Everyone needs a sense of purpose, whatever that looks like to you; as you probably realise, that's a very personal thing. You need a belief that what you're doing is important and that you can make a difference in the world. Making the effort to find your own unique purpose in life could be one of the most important actions you take during your lifetime; that's if you don't know what it is already – and lucky you if you do.

When you live your life with a sense of deep purpose, it does become a source of happiness, fulfilment and, most importantly, empowerment. This is something I've come to experience myself, and I feel its power on a daily basis. It can transform your life and makes what once seemed impossible into something that's very achievable. What I do know is this: *purpose* is something we discover over time when we do things that we love.

How to find purpose

When you're passionate about certain things in your life and you take consistent actions in those areas, then you start living your life with far greater purpose.

However, even if where you are right now isn't where you want to be at all, and you aren't sure of your purpose either, by asking yourself some important questions, you'll be starting that journey of discovery. You'll be getting closer to what that life could actually look like. It's a stepping stone to a new world and a new future, and it can also be the start of unlocking your potential.

Let's help you get some clarity on your purpose.

 Answer the following (let your writing flow freely in your notebook and don't question your answers; simply write down whatever comes into your head):

» *What are your unique contributions to the world so far?*

Think back on your life from your early years up until now and really reflect on this question. This could be anything from your different jobs, exams, being a parent, work experience when you were young, helping others, volunteering, etc.

» *What are your current skills?*

This can be anything from what you do for work, how great you are with social media, how good you are with people, cooking, playing the piano, strategic thinking, etc.

» *What activities make you feel the most alive and give you the most enjoyment in life?*

» *If you knew that failure wasn't an option, what would you most love to do?*

» *What do you enjoy learning about the most?*

» *What kind of giving is the most rewarding for you?*

» *What are you doing when you experience 'flow'? (Flow is when you lose track of time, and whatever you're doing is seamless, easy and enjoyable.)*

» *If you had all the money in the world, what would you spend your time doing?*

How did you get on? I hope you found these questions useful and that you're now a few steps closer to understanding your purpose and, ultimately, your identity, your values and your reason for doing what you do every day.

Finding your purpose could take you a while to work out, as it did for me; it doesn't happen overnight. Please trust the process of answering the previous questions openly and honestly. You'll know it when you feel it! It should be something you absolutely *love* doing, potentially doesn't feel like work, could serve others and fulfils you to the core; something where you get that excited feeling when you think about it!

The Japanese believe that everyone has an *ikigai*, which is a reason to jump out of bed each morning; i.e. the thing that gives you purpose. Finding your *ikigai* comes from asking yourself what you're good at, what you love, what the world needs and what you can be paid for, which in turn gives you passion, a mission in life, a vocation and a profession!

If you're short on time, perhaps jot a few of these ideas down (in your notebook) before you go to sleep and then, in the morning, read through what you wrote and add any thoughts that may have come up overnight. The subconscious mind is always busy at night, and you'd be surprised at what might be revealed in your notes in the morning. If you're a busy mum, try to find 5 minutes here and there to write out your thoughts if you can; there's no time limit to this exercise. The more thought you put into it, the more powerful it becomes.

My purpose became clearer after I created a vision board in November 2017 (I tell the story in more detail starting on page 123); I remember telling my friend Grace excitedly that I thought I had found something that was going to make me really happy, and I was really excited to start showing other people the power of vision boarding, as it had impacted me in such a fundamental way.

Values

The Cambridge Dictionary definition of 'values' is "the beliefs people have, especially about what is right and wrong and what is most important in life, that control their behaviour".[108] As I said earlier, our values define how we behave in life.

It's important for us to reflect on our values, because they guide our behaviour in our work, social and home lives. They drive our beliefs, attitudes and behaviours. Again, I wasn't aware of my values and hadn't even really thought about or written down what my values were until 2018, when I worked with a coach. I came to understand that, when we think of our values, we should think of what's at the core of our existence: What are the words that encompass how we present ourselves to the world (and to ourselves) and how we react to different situations? What do we believe passionately and wholeheartedly in?

When I was training to be an NLP practitioner (under Steve Payne, see page 211 in *Further Resources* for details), we talked a lot about every human being having a different map of the world: each of us is made up so differently, depending on the upbringing we've had and our influences and experiences during our lives. Learning that people can have very different values from yours can help you to better understand others.

Values are important because they can help us to predict each other's choices, and they can help us avoid misunderstandings, frustration and distrust. Comprehending that other people prioritise a different set of values, which guide them toward different decisions, may help you to better understand that their choices may be dissimilar to yours, but they may be right for them.

Values also can direct us to achieve our goals.

Here are some examples of personal values in life:

* Fun (with friends and family) – It's important that you spend time with your friends and family and have fun with them.

* Lifelong learning – Learning and growth is important to you (this could be reading, taking courses, etc.).

* Contribution – It's important that you contribute something to the world, help people and make a positive difference to yourself and others (this could be volunteering, serving others, etc.).

* Kindness – If we truly live by the value of kindness, that means offering it to everyone (including ourselves) and not just when it's easy, convenient or beneficial for us to do so.

* Honesty – You believe in being truthful, honest and sincere with yourself and others.

Obviously, yours may look completely different!

 Here are some questions that will get you thinking more about your values (again, please let your writing flow freely when giving your answers in your notebook, be honest and write until you can't write any more for each one):

» *What energises you?*

» *What do you spend most of your time on?*

» *What and who inspires you on a daily basis?*

» *What do you fill your personal space with?*

» *What do you spend your money on?*

» *Where are you most organised?*

» *What do you think and daydream about most?*

» *What do you like to talk about the most?*

» *Where are you most reliable in life?*

» *What lights you up?*

So, how did you get on? You may have found that you're repeating answers to a lot of the questions, which could be a sign that it's one of your highest values.

What are the values that appear in your answers the most often? Prioritise them, so your most frequent / highest core value is at the top and the least frequent / lowest is last on the list. If you aren't sure whether you're prioritising them correctly, ask yourself what you spend the most time on.

Interestingly, when writing this book I redid this exercise and realised that there are values that are really important to me that I need to focus on more. Your top-three core values should be the ones that make you the most happy.

You may also notice that there are things in your life right now that frustrate you and are nowhere near being in line with your values. This could be your work or people you spend time with, for example.

Your highest values will most likely change over time. That's fine; you can redo this exercise every few months.

Taking some quality time to figure out what your top values in life are will be one of the most important decisions you'll ever make:

- ✓ This could mean the difference between being in a job that you hate and finding work you truly love to do.

- ✓ Your life will have much more meaning.

- ✓ You'll feel less overwhelmed, less frustrated and less disillusioned with life.

- ✓ You'll start doing things that really make you very happy.

If you're struggling to pick your core values, there's a list provided by The Happiness Planner that you should check out (see page 212 in *Further Resources* for details). An alternative list can be found by googling "core values list", and you can then use as a prompt one of the many lists suggested. Having a maximum of 10 core values is good, and remember to put them in order of priority and keep on working on those top three!

Vision boards

I have mentioned vision boards a few times in my book so far, and they are one of my greatest passions. Creating a vision board helps in the process of getting clear on what you want out of life and, later on, finding the reason why you want it so badly. If you don't have a plan in life, you may end up somewhere you'd rather not be, and it's sometimes pretty hard to figure it all out by yourself. Creating a vision board is also a chance to dream, perhaps remembering all of those forgotten hopes and aspirations, and then to embark on making them happen.

What a vision board is

The Dictionary.com definition of a 'vision board' is "a collage of pictures, text, and other items that represent and affirm one's dreams and ambitions, created to help visualise and focus on one or more specific aspirations".[109]

A vision board can also be described as a powerful tool that brings your goals and aspirations to life. It can be a board, a piece of paper, a piece of card, a pinboard, foamboard of any shape or size, or you can create your very own scrapbook.

The board ends up being a physical representation of a goal or goals that you're aiming to achieve over the next year, pushing you towards all of those pictures, words and phrases that end up on your board. The brain remembers images 65% better than words, so looking at a vision board daily keeps you on track and heading towards your goals way quicker than just writing a list.

Your brain is sorting through thousands of bits of information every second of every day, similar to how Google works. The brain then makes a decision, based on thoughts and emotions, regarding what it gives its attention to and what it lets go. A vision board is a very clever tool, because when you look at all the pictures, words and phrases on your board, this directs your brain to what it needs to remember and focus on. The neuroscientific term for this is 'value-tagging'. I highly recommend reading neuroscientist Dr Tara Swart's book *The Source*, which has a whole chapter on what she calls 'action boards', which are Tara's version of vision boards.[110]

Not all my goals get completed every year, but I'd say 95% of them do. They evolve, change and sometimes get carried over to the next year; if I want the goal badly enough, it'll happen (though fear gets in the way sometimes). When that fear does get in the way, I write down my fear in my notebook and look at the evidence. What's stopping me doing it? What's getting in the way? Is there evidence why it isn't possible (usually not!)? Am I letting my thoughts take over? Try some tapping, talk it through with somebody, and use *Chapter 4* as a guide for planning and making it happen. Or get in touch with me!

Why vision boards? My story

At the beginning of 2017, I started following, reading and watching various motivational speakers, trainers and coaches online, as well as reading their books. They included Jack Canfield, Jake Ducey, Marie Forleo, Marissa Peer, Mindvalley and Vishen Lakhiani, T. Harv Eker, Tony Robbins, and a few others. All of them mentioned vision boards at some point, and I was curious to discover what vision boards were.

By November 2017, after about 10 months of doing my morning routine, and with a half-marathon completed and many pounds shed, I was ready (with renewed gusto, self-esteem and confidence), itching to know more and wanting to create my very own vision board.

I ordered the e-book *The Complete Guide to Vision Boards* by Christine Kane. This book has been an enormous part of my life transformation. I can safely say that if it hadn't been for this book and creating that first vision board, my life would still be pretty ordinary, unexciting and unfulfilling. In fact, reflecting on this now, looking at the vision board I created that month and what I then went on to do using vision boards really illustrates just how powerful they are.

The vision board took a week to create, done over a number of evenings. On my vision board was a jumble of images, words and phrases: the words "own an audience" (more about this soon), a picture of a group of runners (I carried on running that year), pictures of a Greek island and books together (I had a week in Mykonos reading books; in particular, one on sleep!), a picture of lots of bicycles (I took up cycling again and took my bike away for weekends), a picture of lots of green space (I walked a lot and discovered new places), a picture to depict adventure (I ended up taking a month off at the end of the year and having loads of adventures), the words "new you" (I carried on building my confidence and discovering a 'new me'), and right in the middle of the board, an image of a woman (which represented me) speaking publicly.

I absolutely didn't plan on having that picture of me as a public speaker on the vision board when I started creating it. It was one of my biggest fears! However, as those who have created vision boards will know, you may well end up with goals and dreams on there that you least expected and that may mean you stepping out of your comfort zone – writing this book, for example! Perhaps it may be a dream that has been buried for years or your subconscious telling you what you need right now in your life.

Literally a week later, I realised what the image of a woman speaking publicly in the middle of my vision board represented: Christine Kane, the lady I had learnt how to make a vision board from, was running a 6-week course on how to teach vision boarding, and my intuition said that I should just go for it! So I signed up for that course to learn how to teach vision boarding from the guru herself. I was terrified.

Thankfully, a friend came to the rescue, and I got an offer of six free coaching sessions. This was my first experience with coaching, and I was lucky enough to be coached by an incredible mindset coach (in training) called Laura Deschivanovits, whom I'd highly recommend. Experiences at school in my childhood had given me a phobia of public speaking and issues with confidence, but in her role as my coach, Laura cleverly unravelled those limiting beliefs, which I realised were just negative thoughts trying to sabotage my progress and to keep me safe and secure.

In February 2018, just 3.5 months after creating my first vision board, I held my first 5-hour vision board workshop. It was an absolute dream come true, with 10 lovely individuals – some of whom were supportive friends there to cheer me on – and I can still remember how I felt at the end of that day, after everything had gone smoothly and I had managed to remember everything (well nearly everything!) I was meant to say and do. I felt elated and ecstatic. Boundaries had been pushed, comfort zones had been conquered, and I was very happy. This had been big-dream stuff, and there I was, ticking one of them off my list. If I could achieve that, then anything was possible!

I didn't go on to give up my job back then, but I ran the workshops in parallel with my freelance business-development work (mainly running one a month at weekends), and I loved them all. These workshops then led me to study neuroscience and brain health with Dr Sarah McKay. Neuroscience is one of my biggest fascinations and passions; as a result, I went on to qualify as an NLP coach and practitioner (I talk about the value of coaching in *Chapter 5*).

At the time of writing this book, my workshops have helped over 320 individuals get clarity around what they want out of life, using a 12-step process I've developed over the last 3.5 years of running these workshops.

I now run a variety of vision board workshops for participants to gain clarity, which specialise in different life areas: career, family, business and life. To find out more about my vision board workshops, please visit my website: **www.themotivationclinic.co.uk.**

Why a vision board is beneficial

The whole process of creating a vision board is massively cathartic. Firstly, you dedicate valuable and special time to concentrate on yourself for a few hours, which most of us never do.

Our lives are so congested and overflowing. We wake up, we work and we have our chores. We have limited flexibility in our daily environments, and we can become almost robotic over time; that's one major reason that most people feel stuck in life. They're exhausted and overworked, they've lost touch with their creative side, and they always come last on their to-do list.

Creating a vision board gets you unstuck. It's also an opportunity to dream about having a better life, a fulfilling career, a successful business, a wonderful relationship, great health and a really enjoyable lifestyle.

It's also an opportunity to jot down on paper the jumble of thoughts that we usually have going round in our heads. Some of those thoughts may be hopes and dreams for a better future that you've never allowed yourself to have.

Finally, what happens in the brain during the process of creating the vision board is essentially a 'positive-emotion booster'. Simply going through the process step by step – which can involve determining intention; journalling; meditation;

flicking through magazines; cutting and sorting through images, words and phrases; visualising; and creating your very own vision board – provides a positive emotional space that energises the brain, as well as producing a lovely dopamine hit!

Vision boards alone don't get you to your goals; you have to be prepared to put in the work, but don't let this stop you from thinking big.

There have been hundreds of success stories from my workshops – books published, beekeeping businesses formed, new homes purchased in new locations, appearances made in the press, health and bodies transformed, careers developed and much, much more!

What you need to create a vision board:

- ✓ Time
- ✓ Space
- ✓ A board, a piece of card or paper, a pinboard, etc.
- ✓ A glue stick
- ✓ Scissors
- ✓ At least 10 assorted magazines
- ✓ An image of yourself to stick in the middle of the board

How to create a vision board:

- ✓ Have fun with it.
- ✓ Get clear on what you want to achieve over the next year (ask yourself how you want to be, what you want to do and what you want to have).

✓ Write down your thoughts (in your notebook) until you can't write any more.

✓ Flick through the magazines.

✓ Pick out pictures and text that resonate with you and that are associated with or represent your goals.

✓ Arrange them into different sections of the board, each representing an area of your life (put the image of yourself in the middle of the board). These are the sections to include:

* Health and recreation

* Work and career

* Finances

* Home environment

* Personal growth

* Travel

* Family and friends

* Community

* Spirituality / religion

✓ Lastly, stick everything onto your vision board and place it in a prominent place in your home where you're going to be able to see it multiple times a day. This could be your kitchen, bedroom or sitting room, for example. Take a photo of your board and keep it as a screen saver and wallpaper for your mobile phone and computer / laptop.

Think of your vision board as being something that evolves. Things can change throughout the year. You may achieve some of the goals on there, so you can replace them with other goals by sticking images on top of what may not be resonating any more. Be open to changes in what you want to achieve. For example, if your goal is to go vegan, don't beat yourself up if you're more of a vegetarian after six months or so.

If you're feeling stuck, overwhelmed and not sure what direction to take next, then creating a vision board is a brilliant, positive process to go through. It'll inspire you, motivate you, excite you, and give you a future vision and belief that anything is possible!

You'll be able to see clearly for the first time in a long time, and the vision board will act as an anchor to keep you motivated and focused.

Be prepared to rediscover forgotten dreams, unearth dreams you didn't even know you had and achieve incredible things!

"Choose a job you love, and you will never have to work a day in your life."

- Confucius

Conclusion

Now we've come to the end of *Chapter 3*, finding your why, your existence in life, your purpose, your values and your vision for the future. As a reminder, in 5 years' time, if you look back on your life right now, would you be proud and excited about what you're doing? Is it meaningful, does it bring you joy, and are you happy and fulfilled?

How did you get on with the different exercises? Are you clear or much clearer on your purpose and your values? And did you manage to create a vision board?

Key points:

» Purpose means having something to live for, a goal or a set of long-term goals that drives us forwards. Without it, we can feel lost at sea.

» Our values define how we behave in life. They influence our behaviour in our work, social and home lives, and they form our beliefs, attitudes and behaviours. What words can we use to describe how we present ourselves to the world (and to ourselves) and respond to various situations? What do we believe passionately and wholeheartedly in?

» A vision board is a powerful tool that brings your goals and aspirations to life. Without a clear future vision, knowing where we're heading and what we want to achieve out of life, we can flounder.

CHAPTER FOUR

STEP 4: PLAN IT!

My hope at this point in the book is that you'll have carved out some time to create your very own vision board. Congratulations if you've created your future vision using the guidance of the previous chapter and now have a vision board placed somewhere significant and in view in your home.

 If not, I'd urge you to give it a go, or see if I'm running a workshop and come to that – just visit **www.themotivationclinic.co.uk** for times and places.

Some of your life goals (hopefully, now identified) and dreams may be overwhelming. The larger and loftier the goal, the more overwhelmed it could make you feel, and you may not be able to even contemplate achieving it. This is said from experience! But with the right planning, support and encouragement, my motto is "Anything is possible".

The first step is to break your goal down. Think about the smaller goals that are steps on the way to achieving your bigger aim. Sometimes, our big goals are a bit vague, such as "I want to be healthier". Breaking these down helps us to be more specific, so a smaller goal might be "to go running regularly" or even "to be able to run around the park in 20 minutes without stopping". Write down your smaller goals and try to set some dates to do these by too. Having several smaller goals makes each of them a bit easier to achieve and gives us a feeling of success along the way, which also makes it more likely that we'll stay on track towards our bigger goal.

Visualise how it'll make you feel once you've achieved the goal, and use affirmations along the way (for example, "I'm so happy and grateful that I'm now fit and healthy, and I feel great").

Chunking your goal

Let's use "I want to be healthier" as an example goal. This may seem like a daunting task at first, as it did for me at the beginning of 2017, but with the right planning, you can make it feel far less intimidating, completely doable and actually enjoyable.

When I was training to be an NLP coach and practitioner (see 'Learning – Open your mind' on page 49 in *Chapter 1* for more details), we covered coaching our clients through planning their goals. I loved the analogy of thinking of the goal itself as a massive storage box and then all the steps you'd need to take to achieve this goal as shoeboxes that can all be placed in the box in a certain order. However you like to think of it, I believe considering the steps as chunks is the most useful concept.

Brain dumping and creating a list

Brain dumping is an action to get all of the ideas from your head down on paper or digitally. This is a safe place to jot down whatever you need to help organise your life or clear your head, and to help prioritise your goals, tasks and chunks. It involves removing from your mind the thoughts where you're overthinking and then placing them somewhere else. This can facilitate you living more freely throughout each day, as the things that are troubling you (that is, your massive goal plus other things you want to achieve) are being resolved.

Going back to our example goal of "I want to be healthier", these ideas could be the following:

» *"I want to lose weight."*

» *"I want to drink less alcohol."*

» *"I want to be more organised with my meals and make them healthy."*

» *"I want to make healthy, green juices every morning."*

» *"I want to factor regular exercise into my life (running, walking, going to the gym, etc.)."*

Creating lists using notebooks, Trello, Google Docs or MS Word

Use your notebook for making a list or, as an alternative, I use Trello when list building and chunking digitally. Trello is a web-based, list-making application that I love, and I highly recommend you give it a go if you don't use it already. If my clients are keen to use this system, I take them through some basic training. As another option, you could use Google Docs, which is like a MS Word document, but it's cloud based, and you can easily share the file and edit it if required. These days, you can also do something similar with MS Word (if the document is stored on OneDrive or SharePoint) and it's also perfectly fine to use offline.

Think of every task that you may need to do to achieve this goal. Enlist a friend or colleague to brainstorm with you too. Two heads are definitely better than one.

A brainstorm could come up with a list such as this:

- » *How often am I going to exercise every week?*

- » *Look up recipes for green juices.*

- » *Who can I buddy up with to get more healthy, so I'm accountable?*

- » *Speak to my friend Emma who's always super organised with meal planning/healthy meals.*

- » *What books do I have that promote health that I could use?*

Post-Its, paper and Magic Charts

If digital isn't your thing, then you may find using paper easier. Sometimes, the act of writing on a piece of paper the list of things that come into your head is just as good. Write the subject or goal at the top – in this case, "I want to be healthier." You can use Post-Its, pieces of paper or a product I recommend called Magic Charts, which are very clever, adhesive, whiteboard-sized, recyclable pieces of paper that you can stick up on a wall (they stick to all interior surfaces). They are completely genius and one of my favourite tools to use when brainstorming.

Mind mapping

Another method used in planning is mind mapping (see Figure 1 for an example). Mind mapping is a graphical way to represent a certain idea, concept or goal. It's a visual tool that helps to structure information, so you're better able to analyse and generate new ideas. Information in a mind map is organised in a way that reflects how the brain actually works.

You start with the subject in the middle, and then you start writing whatever comes into your head that relates to the subject or goal in the middle. Seeing it structured in this way can really get your creative juices flowing, and ideas come that you may not have thought about previously. It's all the better if you can to do it in a group or with one other person.

You can either draw your own mind map or use a digital version. There are plenty of free applications available, including Canva, Coggle and Miro.

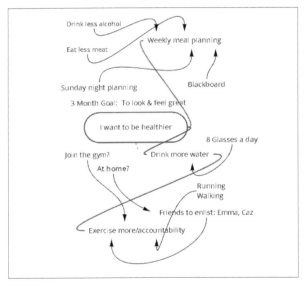

Figure 1. Mind map example (using Miro)

Example of planning

Let's use the goal of "I want to be healthier" as an example to illustrate how planning around this would work.

These are some useful questions to ask yourself (chunks):

» *What is the name of the goal? (In this case, "I want to be healthier")*

» *As yourself: What? Who? Why? When? Where? How?*

» *What can I do to become healthier?*

» *Who could help me to get healthier? Who could join me on this mission?*

» *Why do I want to be healthier? What's my end goal? What does becoming healthier actually mean to me?*

» *When do I want to get healthier by? Do I have an end date in mind?*

» *Where could I do something to help me get healthier? Does it mean joining a gym, working out at home, exercising in the local park, taking up a sport, etc.?*

» *How can I get healthier? How many times and for how long will I exercise every week? How will I plan my meals?*

Inevitably, what happens as you go along with this type of planning is that other thoughts and ideas then start flowing. The beauty of brainstorming and writing your ideas down (in your notebook) is that your subconscious will be busy in the background thinking up new and innovative ideas you may not have considered before.

Your brain is your supercomputer, helping you to progress the achievement of your goals and dreams. The better the planning, the better the results. My method has always been taking baby steps: actionable, small steps or chunks that, in the long run, add up to large goals. It's an exciting process!

Getting cracking on the goal using your chunked plan

You should now have lots of ideas laid out in chunks, either in your notebook, Trello, Google Docs, MS Word, or on Post-Its, paper or Magic Charts, perhaps in the form of a mind map. Next, it's time to plot out your different chunks/subjects over time.

Consider this a fun process to go through. Thinking about the topic "I want to get healthier" and all the answers to the questions in the 'Example of planning' section on page 136, you should then plan out your actions over time.

For this example, let's say that you're going to give yourself three months to "get healthier" and this means the following:

- ✓ Drinking alcohol less often (on only 2 nights a week) and a smaller amount in total

- ✓ Eating vegetarian on 3 days a week and meat/fish on 4 days a week

- ✓ Exercising 5 days a week (running 3 kilometres twice a week and taking a brisk 30-minute walk three times a week)

A good old MS Excel spreadsheet (or Google Sheet) is great for this planning exercise (see Figure 2 for an example). I use either an MS Excel spreadsheet or a pie chart (or both) with my clients, depending on whether they like using MS Excel or not.

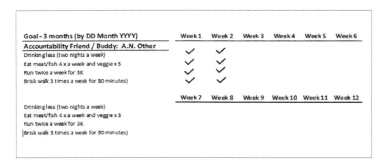

Figure 2. Spreadsheet planning example

This very basic chart can be adjusted to cover all of the weeks you wish to include, so that you can tick them off. Print out this list and put it on the fridge in your kitchen to remind yourself what you're trying to achieve. Even if your particular goal isn't around health, the fridge is still a good place to put a list as a reminder and a prompt to keep you motivated, or you could find another place in your home where you'll see it every day. Put reminders in your calendar or diary (both paper and digital). You could also cut out of a magazine an image that represents achieving the overall goal and stick that up alongside your list.

At the end of every week, reward yourself for achieving that week's goals.

I talk about accountability buddies in *Chapter 5*, but find a good friend, colleague or acquaintance who can work with you to make this happen. They can either assist you by having the same goal to achieve themself or you can check in with them every week to make sure you're keeping on track with your goal.

Time management / productivity hacks

A whopping 95% of women and some men at my vision board workshops state that procrastination is one of their biggest challenges, and it's not surprising! We all suffer from this debilitating habit, but it's important for us to understand why we humans sabotage ourselves in this way.

Earlier in the book, I wrote that a human being can produce 60,000–80,000 thoughts in one day, which is an average of 2,500–3,300 thoughts per hour. The mind is like a butterfly that flies from one flower to another, never standing still. Sometimes, this endless flow of thoughts is tiring and exhausting, especially when we're anxious or worried about something, perhaps what we're trying to achieve.

Up to 80% of the thoughts we have each day are negative, fearful and downright unhelpful! We often procrastinate because we're afraid of failing at the task we need to complete, and our own mind also loves to tell us that we can't do something! It likes to keep us safe.

It's important to keep in mind that we each have the ability to control our thoughts, install any thought into our mind, remove any thought from our mind and, most importantly, choose our own thoughts.

I've learnt over time that if you aren't looking forward to doing something or are fearful of it, using affirmations (see 'Affirmations – Make it true' section on page 30) is a great way of retraining your brain to think in a different way.

Going back to our example of "I want to be healthier", there are systems that you can put in place for yourself that will make it much easier to achieve your goals. Don't let your mind sabotage your progress and leave you in procrastination freefall.

Plan your week on a Sunday

You'll be pleased to know that you absolutely can reframe (see next paragraph) and encourage yourself when you're not feeling motivated to do something. Sanae Floyd, an incredible coach whom I worked with for a few months (see page 211 in *Further Resources* for her contact details), taught me this fantastic system of planning your week on a Sunday evening. If you spend 20 minutes looking at your diary for the week ahead and mentally getting ready for the different things that you need to achieve or do, you'll be better prepared and be able to really hit the ground running when you sit at your desk on Monday.

She also suggests using an alter ego name for the "new you", such as "Dynamic Health Junkie" (that is, representing the person you'll be when you are actioning all these changes). Imagine yourself completing all the goals and consider how that's going to make you feel. This reframes, encourages and motivates you, particularly when you say to yourself "I am a dynamic health junkie!" (said out loud with energy!).

So let's look at those goals again:

- ✓ Drinking alcohol less often (on only 2 nights a week) and a smaller amount in total – You could make sure that you don't buy alcohol until the weekend, for example, and limit it to purchasing a half-bottle of wine.

- ✓ Eating vegetarian on 3 days a week and meat/fish on 4 days a week – On Sunday night you can decide what you're going to cook each night of the week and plan ahead (and decide when you'll go shopping for food, what you'll buy and schedule all this in your diary).

- ✓ Exercising 5 days a week (running 3 kilometres twice a week and taking a brisk 30-minute walk three times a week) – Again, on a Sunday night, you could plan which days you're going to exercise on and what exercise you will do on each of those days. A top tip for this is to do your exercise first thing in the morning and leave your kit out the night before, so you figuratively trip over it the next morning; that means there are no excuses for not doing it! Enlist a friend / accountability buddy to walk or exercise with you to make it easier, or call each other for support.

"The journey of a thousand miles begins with a single step."

– Lao Tzu

Set an intention

Setting an intention is a commitment to how you want your day or week to pan out. When you're intentional about something, your focus is in the moment: who you are, what you do and why you do it.

 For the goals listed in the previous section, your intention might be this (write this down in your notebook on a Sunday night):

» "I look forward to checking in with [accountability buddy] on Friday morning to confirm that I've had an alcohol-free week, I've cooked delicious meat-free meals on 3 days, I've run 3 kilometres on Monday, and I've walked briskly for 30 minutes on Wednesday and Friday mornings. I'm a more energised, positive and healthy person, and I'm loving that the pounds seem to be dropping off easily."

Put your phone in another room

Your mobile phone is probably one of the biggest distractions with respect to progress that you have in your home. Probably my most important piece of advice for when you want focus and give your attention to the task ahead is to get rid of any temptation to scroll through social media or to use your phone in another way and you can do this by removing it from the room completely. Trust me, you'll thank me for this little (or mighty!) piece of advice.

Use a timer

In *Chapter 1*, I described my amazing, little 60-minute countdown timer that now sits proudly next to my laptop. This great time-management tool is useful to use in conjunction with either the Pomodoro Technique (mentioned on page 75 in *Chapter 1*) (working for 25 minutes then taking a 5-minute break, with each work session being called a 'pomodoro') or my favourite method of doing 52 minutes of work and then taking a 17-minute break.

As a reminder, these techniques help you to resist all of those self-interruptions and retrain your brain to focus while working. Each pomodoro or work session is dedicated to one task, and each break is a chance to reset yourself and bring your attention back to what you should be working on. I've used the 52/17 method to write this book with amazing success, so I can highly recommend it.

Don't forget that your brain will love the reward you give it after the work chunk: a walk, a meditation, a breathing exercise, sleep, drinking a glass of water, contacting a friend you haven't been in touch with for a while, making a cup of tea or coffee, or reading a page of a book.

The breaks increase your productivity and creativity, and help you to process and retain information. Working for long stretches without breaks leads to stress and exhaustion. Taking breaks refreshes your mind, replenishes your mental resources and helps you become more creative.

Research reveals that 'aha moments' come more often to those who take regular breaks.[111] Other evidence suggests that taking regular breaks raises employees' levels of engagement, which, in turn, is highly correlated with productivity.[112]

Remember your why – Affirmations

Finally, if your motivation is waning at any point, have an affirmation written on a Post-It that you can see to keep yourself focused; include why you're trying to achieve this goal and how it's going to make you feel at the end of it. For example, "I'm so happy and grateful that being healthy makes me feel great, inside and out. I have more energy to enjoy life, I've lost half a stone, I have better mental health and I'm able to fit into my clothes again."

Conclusion

So how did you get on with working on and planning your goals? This part can be really exciting – keep thinking of the outcome, the opportunity and the possibility that achieving this goal may bring. In the next chapter, I'll talk about how having accountability will get you closer to achieving your goals and help you do so faster.

Key points:

» Brainstorm your goal. Write everything out that you can think of that relates to your goal.

» Think to yourself: What? Who? Why? When? Where? How?

» Remember the box analogy. Imagine all the elements that make up achieving your goal as shoeboxes that can be fitted into a bigger box.

» Give your goal a deadline.

» Plan your goal using a timeline, diary or spreadsheet.

» Stick your plan up on your fridge or somewhere else where you can see it often.

» Supercharge your week by planning on a Sunday, making things easy for yourself and setting an intention for your week ahead.

» Share your goal with a friend or accountability buddy.

» Try not to get distracted by scrolling through social media on your mobile phone.

» Finally, remember why you want to achieve this goal so much and how it's going to make you feel when you've achieved it.

"A goal without a plan is just a wish."

— Antoine de Saint-Exupéry

CHAPTER FIVE

STEP 5: ASSISTANCE

This book was written to aid women in getting unstuck and unlocking undiscovered potential, so they can transform their lives into ones that are fulfilled and happy. I must stress again that I'm not telling you to do all these things; I'm just illustrating what has worked for me, many people I know and my clients.

The previous chapters are all about putting in place the building blocks, pillars or stepping stones to that new life; these are the foundations to keep you strong when you may be having a difficult day. It's completely normal to have an off day, or week, particularly considering the COVID-19 pandemic, having your hormones all over the place or being impacted by other factors in your life that may be out of your control. My hope is that, when you're having one of those tough days or weeks, first and foremost, you'll be open about how you're feeling with your loved ones and share your pain; remember the toxic positivity I mentioned earlier (see page 14 in the *Introduction*)? More on this as a reminder later. Additionally, you can flick through this book and the notes you've made in your notebook to remind yourself of the methods that can bring you back to a more positive mindset and away from despair.

Many a time, I've found myself in this position of trying to remember all the things that make me feel good, so that's why I wanted it all in one place – which is now this book.

Maybe you can put some of your favourite music on, give that friend a call, look at your vision board, get out in nature, or remind yourself of your purpose and values, and then remember where you've come from and where you're heading. Most importantly, think about your exciting future!

It can be hard going it alone, and most of us need support, encouragement and accountability from others to keep us focused and motivated. That's why I've included this chapter to give options for different types of help and assistance that have worked for me in the past and that I also know works for many others.

When I look back at what I've achieved over the last few years of working freelance and running a small business, it would have been so much harder had it not been for the friends, family, coaches, mentors, networks, accountability buddies and virtual assistants (VAs) whom I've talked to and worked with, plus having my vision board to guide me and keep me motivated, and my morning routine to act as a pillar of strength and positivity.

If you managed to create a vision board (see page 127 in *Chapter 3* for details) – or even if you didn't, but you instead managed to think about and write down in your notebook what you want to achieve over the next year, and there happen to be some big dreams on that list of yours – then you may be wondering how you're going to tackle achieving those dreams or goals with or without your plan.

Research[113] has shown that we're more likely to achieve our goals (65% more) if we're held accountable to somebody, whether it's an accountability buddy, mentor, coach or group. Your chance of reaching a goal successfully rises to 95% when you establish an ongoing appointment with your accountability partner or group. The next sections give an outline of the different assistance methods that are easily accessible and can help you get closer to achieving your goals in a more structured and quicker way, whatever your situation.

Friends and family

In *Chapter 2*, I talked about how important our environment is and, in particular, how our friends and family can help us deal with stress, help us make better lifestyle choices that keep us strong, and allow us to rebound from health issues and disease more quickly. Our friends and family are also there when we need support and encouragement.

At the beginning of this book (see page 14), I discussed toxic positivity and the damage that we can do to our mental health if we don't share how we are feeling. The same goes for when we have goals that we want to achieve: sharing our ideas and dreams with the right loved ones can be of major benefit, and it's reassuring to receive their support and encouragement.

However, it may be that you don't want to share your goals and dreams with your nearest and dearest, so the following options could be a good alternative.

Coaching

The essence of coaching and being a coach is to help a person change in the way they wish to and to assist them to go in the direction they want to. Coaching supports a person at every level in becoming who they want to be, and at the same time, it builds awareness, empowers choice and leads to change. A coach helps each client to achieve their personal best and to produce the results they want in their personal and professional lives.

The Association of Coaching defines coaching as "A collaborative solution-focused, results orientated and systematic process in which the coach facilitates the enhancement of work performance, life experience, self-directed learning and personal growth of the coachee."[114]

The Life Coach Directory explains coaching is the following:[115]

> *Coaching is a process where a coach supports a coachee to make a change, learn something new or achieve goals. This process happens through conversation, and can take place face-to-face, over the phone, or online.*

> *The ultimate aim of a coach is to help the coachee make progress in a certain area of their life, at work or to overcome a problem they're struggling with.*

Coaching is relevant for you if you run your own business, you have an idea for a business, you are in employment, you are currently not working, you are a student or you are a busy parent.

Coaching has traditionally been associated with sports. Every top athlete has a coach. In the last few years, coaching has become applicable to many other areas, including business and life. It's quite normal for someone to see a coach to help them achieve their life and work goals.

Coaching is a partnership between coach and client. The coach need not be an expert in their clients' field of work.

I mentioned earlier in this book that my first coaching experience was with a mindset coach who helped me to overcome my fears of public speaking, so I could command the room for my first vision board workshop. Thank you again, Laura! She gave me the gift of 6 hours of brilliant coaching. Without those 6 hours, perhaps I wouldn't be writing these words now? Would I have let my fears overcome me, forgotten the idea of running vision board workshops and taken the easy way out, instead of facing my demons and stepping out of my comfort zone. I think I have so much to thank Laura for!

As you can see, there's so much power behind great coaching. The role of a coach is to listen and ask brilliant questions (not to tell somebody what to do), so the person being coached can live a life of opportunity, success, happiness and fulfilment.

If, when you come away from a coaching session, your thinking and learning have benefitted, and you go on to take action, then you've been coached well. This was my experience, and that's why I consider coaching to be such a key element in our personal development and chose to feature it in this book.

I happen to think working with a coach is one of the most powerful things you can do for your development as a human being. It has affected me in such a profound way – so much so that I've gone on to qualify as a coach. I can't now imagine not having a coach or being part of a coaching group.

How coaching is different from counselling

Counselling is reactive and problem focused; coaching is proactive and solution focused. Counselling is about the past; coaching relates to where you are now and your future (goal based). Counselling and therapy move a person from dysfunctional to functional; coaching moves someone from functional to exceptional.

A belief that underpins coaching is that we already have the answers we need within us. A coach's role is to help their clients or coachees to find the answers. As I said earlier, an excellent coach asks pertinent questions, listens actively, observes and reflects back. When these techniques are used, the coachee gains greater self-awareness and often obtains insight they didn't have previously. Having a non-biased, non-judgemental person available to provide focused attention gives the coachee space to understand how to move forwards.

Some coaches, including me, use NLP techniques in their work, and some will use tools such as journalling and meditation to support conversational work. There are many different models that can be used within coaching, and it's very much up to the coach to decide which tools they'll use and what approaches they'll take.

Coaching often focuses on goal setting to ensure progress is being made. Action points from a session will give the coachee an indication of what steps they need to take to keep moving forwards between sessions.

The benefits of coaching

There are multiple benefits of coaching, including the following:

- ✓ It provides you with a source of accountability.
- ✓ It can help you define your purpose.
- ✓ It helps you learn, rather than being taught.
- ✓ It improves your confidence and sense of self-worth.
- ✓ It provides you with clarity, direction and focus.
- ✓ It raises your self-awareness.
- ✓ It enables you to change certain behaviours.
- ✓ It helps you to learn a new skill.

With an emphasis on forward progression, unlocking potential and achieving goals, it's no surprise that many people describe coaching as being life-changing.

Coaching (and using vision boards) has been life-changing for me too. I've gained so much knowledge about myself, and I've overcome so many barriers, many of which I've since forgotten about now (though I still have some to get past) but that seemed like mountains at the time.

How I coach

At the time of writing, I've worked with more than 320 women in total to help them find clarity and direction in their work and life using vision boards. In my work with women on a 1-2-1 basis, I use various coaching methods (including vision boards) that I've learnt and developed since November 2017.

My training, experience and coaching methods originate from the following:

» 1990 to the present – Working in various corporate roles, which includes senior management positions.

» Nov/Dec 2017 – Learning (from the expert Christine Kane) how to facilitate vision board workshops and how to coach individuals through the process of vision boarding.

» Feb 2018 to the present – Coaching individuals and groups at motivation clinics through my powerful '12 Steps to Change' method.

» Aug 2020 – Obtaining a Certificate in Neuroscience and Brain Health from The Neuroscience Academy.

» Feb 2021 – Obtaining the following qualifications: certification as an NLP practitioner, a Diploma in NLP and a Certificate in Professional Coaching Skills with The Academy of Coaching & Training, which is part of The Association of NLP.

My 1-2-1 coaching process starts with a discovery call to work out if my client and I are both matched as individuals, and we'll do a dive into my client's life. It's fundamental that my client and I build a good working relationship that's underpinned by trust, respect and confidentiality.

When we start working together, I can quickly help women go from being stuck, confused, living in chaos and overwhelmed to having clarity and insight around what they want out of their life. I know how it is to feel stuck and woolly, and it's amazing to witness the transformation in others.

Once they have clarity and a renewed sense of direction with it, I help my client to break down their vision into smaller goals and achievable tasks, and I then facilitate the creation of daily practices that will continually move them towards their dreams, unlock their potential, and create a happier and fulfilled life – one that they truly deserve.

I support and encourage my clients to move forwards and grow every step of the way, keeping them motivated and their energy high, and making sure they're putting themselves at the top of their to-do list!

I make notes at every meeting we have, so that there's always a record of what we've discussed; this way, my clients can see what they've achieved between each session and what they'll be accountable for before our next meeting.

Finding a coach

Over the last few years, I've found the various coaches I've worked with organically, either having followed their progress on social media (LinkedIn, Facebook or Instagram) or they've come highly recommended.

As coaching involves an investment in your future and facilitates important decisions, picking the right one shouldn't be taken lightly. Take your time, do your research and make sure they're qualified. Use the time in a discovery call to make sure that you feel right about the relationship and the way the coach works.

There are many different types of coaches, including these:

- » Mindset coach
- » Career coach
- » Life coach
- » Business coach
- » Performance coach
- » Relationship coach
- » Health coach
- » Book coach

Coaching can take place face to face, on the phone, or via Zoom, MS Teams or other similar services.

Is there a cost?

Generally, yes. It may be free if you're able to find somebody who is in training to be a coach, which is what I did with Laura, the first coach I worked with. This is a great opportunity to try out coaching for the first time.

For a trained and qualified professional, prices can range from £40 upwards per session, but coaches tend to give prices on a per-package basis, depending on the extent of your needs. The overall price will be impacted by how many sessions you need and whether you'll need regular check-ups with your coach to confirm you're on track. You may need fewer sessions than someone who's hoping to set long-term goals over a few years.

Coaches may also offer group packages. I took part in a 12-week group coaching programme with an amazing group of women, some of whom I'm still in touch with months later. Group coaching can prove to be a more affordable option to 1-2-1 coaching, and it's also great to have the additional accountability from your fellow group members.

I've included a list of the brilliant coaches I know, some of whom I've worked with, in the 'People' section of *Further Resources* (see page 211).

Mentors

A mentor is a person who's experienced in a particular field or business (perhaps someone who has achieved something remarkable), who shares the benefits of their experience with a person called a mentee. The role of a mentor is usually to help mentees set up an action plan to achieve specific career goals, though a mentor can provide guidance in other areas of a mentee's life as well. They can aid their mentee in stretching their realm of possibility.

A mentor may be relevant for you if you are an entrepreneur, have an idea for a business, are in employment, are currently not working, are a student or are a busy parent.

Mentoring and coaching may use similar skills and approaches, but coaching is short-term and task-based, and mentoring is a longer-term relationship. The difference can be summarised as follows: "a coach has some great questions for your answers; a mentor has some great answers for your questions" (Brefi Group).

A mentor may be a more experienced colleague, associate or a business owner. They could also be someone unrelated to the mentee's employment who takes an interest in their development.

Mentors are usually volunteers (but not always). They may have a long-standing relationship with a mentee or may acquaint themselves with the mentee solely in the course of the mentoring relationship. The common thread is the relationship itself: The mentor will act as a guide and adviser who directs the mentee through a stage of their development process; the mentee is similar to an apprentice who's eager to soak up the mentor's wisdom and advice.

The benefits of mentoring

- ✓ You learn from the experiences of the mentor.
- ✓ You're exposed to new ideas and ways of thinking.
- ✓ You become more empowered.
- ✓ You develop your communication and personal skills.
- ✓ You receive valuable advice around different industries.
- ✓ The mentor can introduce you to others who may be helpful for you to know.
- ✓ They could provide a reference for you.
- ✓ They may alert you to a job prospect.

Being a mentor has its benefits too. As well as the personal satisfaction of sharing their skills and experience with a willing learner, being involved in mentoring also provides some benefits that can reward mentors professionally:

- » It develops their personal leadership and coaching styles.
- » It provides an extension to their professional development record.

» It offers an opportunity to reflect on their own goals and practices.

» It exposes them to fresh perspectives, ideas and approaches.

Some individuals have mentors who they never actually meet face to face, as everything is done virtually.

Finding a mentor

If you think of the people that you admire the most in or outside your industry, these people could potentially be a mentor to you. Send them an email or a message to have a conversation with them. Alternatively, contact them through LinkedIn. I've found in the past that people are flattered to be asked, and if they have time in their diaries and they think you'll be a good fit, they'd be delighted to mentor you.

However, please don't be offended if they say no (this has happened to me)! Remember that people are busy, and it could be that this individual isn't quite the right fit for you anyway. Do your research, and keep it in mind during your search that this is a person whom you admire and could be a great teacher for you.

I've worked with a couple of mentors over the last few years, both of whom I'm extremely grateful to and thankful for. I approached both of the individuals via email, and we then had a conversation on the telephone. Our sessions were scheduled dependent on our time constraints, and I had an extremely positive experience with both. (You know who you are! Thank you!)

Is there a cost?

For the type of mentor I have just described, their mentoring is free, which makes them priceless in more ways than one. Such a mentoring relationship will grow organically through connections within your industry and network. This type of mentor won't be mentoring you for the money; instead, they're driven by the satisfaction of helping another individual or entrepreneur – paying it forwards from a similar experience they had when starting their own business.

However, there are those who do offer mentoring as a business and so will charge you in a similar way to a coach. Engaging such a mentor is still a viable option, but I'd recommend finding the type of mentor I've just described if you can. If you do go down this paid-mentor route, you'll need to use a similar process for choosing one that I've described for picking a coach.

Accountability partner / buddy

Having an accountability partner or buddy is like being in a partnership where you mutually agree to coach each other and provide feedback on a regular basis. This partnership can be with a friend, work colleague or acquaintance. With an accountability partner, you each agree to talk daily, weekly, fortnightly, etc. through feedback sessions where you share wins, discuss your current challenges and set goals together. I've had an accountability partner for a couple of years now, who's a friend and ex-colleague. It has proved to be a great addition to my life (thank you, Rem!).

Accountability partners / buddies are most relevant for you if you run your own business or if you have an idea for a business, but they can also be helpful if you're in employment, unemployed, a student or a busy parent.

As I mentioned earlier, adding a specific accountability partner with whom you check in regularly increases your chance of success to 95%.[116]

It can be hard working alone and running a one-man-band business, so this is somebody you can check in with on a regular basis, for the reasons I mention earlier on the page and to help you generally feel less alone working on your business. They're also useful to give you a kick up the butt and for you to be held accountable for some of your tasks.

I liken my accountability partner to my partner in crime, and having one helps me to be more productive and follow through on some of the projects I may have been putting off. For example, we had a great session together yesterday (at the time of writing), and we've both committed to doing the one task that we had been putting off before we do anything else today!

Every Friday morning, I also run an accountability group where a few of us meet up on Zoom. We talk about what we've achieved that week and then we describe what we're going to accomplish in the time allocated. The alarm then goes on for 52 minutes of work followed by a 17-minute break, and off we go! It's a great system, and it really works!

Finding an accountability partner / buddy

Finding a great accountability partner is as important as having one. Look through your list of immediate friends, colleagues or acquaintances; think about who might be suitable; and then approach them to see if they'd be interested.

When considering who might make a good accountability buddy, there are some special attributes that they need to have, and the following points are a good prompt:

» This person can pull you out of overwhelm and stress and also make you feel motivated.

» This person wants the very best for you.

» This person makes you a better and more successful person.

» This person has lots of experience, so they can guide you in your decisions.

» This person is a sounding board for ideas, and they will be completely honest and constructive with their feedback.

» This person is reliable and always on time for meetups.

It's always a good idea to put the ground rules in place before you and your accountability partner start working with each other. Once this has been done, then you should agree how often you'll be in touch, meet up online, speak on the phone or meet face to face. Schedule it in your diaries.

Working with an accountability partner is a great way to understand your flaws and make room for improvement. They can help you by providing a neutral perspective on the situations you're facing in your life and can help you to understand everything from another person's perspective. With their help, you can make the right decisions and achieve more of your goals.

Is there a cost?

No; accountability partners or buddies are free. You should see this relationship as mutually beneficial, and don't forget how powerful it is to have someone to whom you are accountable for reaching your goals!

Networks and networking

Having a well-established network has become an important part of our lives, particularly during the COVID-19 pandemic. The easiest way to expand and strengthen our network is to build on the relationships with people we already know: family, friends, colleagues and acquaintances.

Throughout the pandemic, natural networks have developed; for example, on Instagram, Facebook groups, and local business and community networks. Networks are relevant for most of us, particularly if you're an entrepreneur or thinking of setting up a business, employed (or even unemployed), a parent or a student, or even if you're elderly.

Having a network or being part of a networking group is beneficial in the following ways and more:

- ✓ Networking is about sharing, not taking; it's a way of forming trust and perhaps finding opportunities to assist others.

- ✓ It can help you to build your confidence. When you put yourself out there and push yourself out of your comfort zone by meeting new people, you build invaluable social skills and self-confidence.

✓   The more you network, the more you'll grow and learn how to make lasting connections.

✓   It can help you to see a different perspective. Try asking for opinions from contacts you trust or admire to help you see things in a new light and overcome blocks that you might not have known how to conquer otherwise.

✓   It's a great opportunity to exchange best-practice knowledge, to learn about your peers' different business techniques and to stay abreast of the latest industry developments.

✓   It helps to build your reputation, particularly if you offer useful information or tips to people who need it.

✓   It helps you to develop and nurture professional relationships.

✓   It can help to create new opportunities for your business, career advancement or personal growth.

I mentioned earlier in this book that I'm not a natural networker, and I know that I'm not alone in that! In fact, for some, the thought of starting a conversation with a stranger at an event incites downright dread.

If you're a business owner who's going to a business networking event, either online or face to face, it's always good to have a pitch for your business at the ready and any discussion points in mind if you know you're going to be in a situation where you'll have the opportunity to meet new people. These conversation points don't have to be all about work: they can be about topics such as hobbies or the event itself. The idea is to get the conversation flowing and to leave room for future meetups and discussions. On that note, don't forget to take business cards with you, so you can swap details easily.

Finding a network

At the time of writing and throughout the COVID-19 pandemic, I've been lucky enough to have attended many online networking events and, more recently, I've been going back to networking face to face.

As I said earlier, as a small-business owner, Instagram has become a supportive network throughout the pandemic, as have smaller groups/networks on Facebook and the LinkedIn community. I'd suggest googling networking events in your area, have a look in your local community magazine or put a message out for recommendations on your local Nextdoor, which is a social networking app that joins together people in the same neighbourhood, allowing you to chat with your neighbours to get local tips, buy and sell items, and more. It has really connected me to my local community throughout the pandemic, and I highly recommend using it.

Additionally, ask your friends, colleagues and acquaintances if they know of any good events, groups or networks that you could be part of; this could also include things that you're interested in outside work!

I can highly recommend a network and community of small-business owners called Inspiration Space. I've now been part of this stimulating network for over two years, and it has taken away the loneliness of working alone on my business, as I know that I have like-minded peers who are just a message, email or phone call away. I've also made very good friends, collaborations and contacts through this network, and I'm very grateful to Liana Fricker (the founder of Inspiration Space) and all the incredible people I've met this way.

Finally, I also recommend Well+Life+Tribe, which is a wellness community and network. I've also made good friends, working partnerships and connections through this network, and I'm grateful to its founder (Kat Vitou) and all of its members.

Is there a cost?

Yes and no. Most networking events charge a fee (per month or per meeting); for face-to-face networking events, this is generally £10–£30 per event, which includes food and drink, but some are considerably more expensive and also include an annual membership fee (these can be in the region of costing £1,500 per year in total). Occasionally, you may find free local networking events too.

For online networking events, those such as LinkedIn Local (I use the free version of LinkedIn at the time of writing), Facebook groups and Instagram groups are free, but there are also paid online networking events too (particularly those run by a national franchise or where a face-to-face group has gone online during the COVID-19 pandemic).

Virtual assistants (VAs)

A VA is a PA who works remotely. They're much in demand with entrepreneurs and online businesses, which engage them for specific tasks, such as social media management, marketing, diary management, event management, bookkeeping and many other services. Some VAs specialise in a specific skill set, and they only perform duties related to those skills.

Using a VA will be most relevant to you if you're running your own business, are considering starting your own business or you run a busy household.

At various points in my life over the last few years, using a VA has been one of the best decisions I've made. Yes, there's an expense to hiring one, but in the long run, you save time on the tasks that perhaps you aren't the best at doing, don't have the right skills set to do or don't really enjoy.

You may also feel overwhelmed with your current workload, are working long hours and want to use your time more productively, or want to decrease your stress levels (and cortisol!), and you can achieve this by working with somebody who knows what they're doing and isn't going to waste the time that you'd probably spend working out how to do the task!

If you're a small-business owner or work in a smaller business that can't afford to hire a full-time member of staff for these sorts of activities, outsourcing different tasks to a VA is a win-win situation in my mind.

This is for the following reasons:

»   VAs can be cost-effective as they tend not be exclusive to you. It's a cheaper way to get added help.

»   An increase in productivity – VAs work without the distractions of an office environment. They dedicate their time to and focus on getting tasks done quickly and efficiently.

»   Flexible working – VAs can work around your schedule, and sometimes work at weekends and in evenings.

»   Improved quality of work – VAs sometimes have a full range of skills that you yourself or other members of your team may not have.

Whether your business is medium-sized or small, it's unlikely that you and your staff have every single skill you need to run it.

Finding a VA

The VAs that I've used in the past are ones I've either met at a networking group, have been referred to or I've organically ended up working with.

My suggestion would be to send a message out to your immediate network of friends, colleagues and acquaintances to ask them if they know of or can recommend a brilliant VA, and you'll then get a recommendation or two and perhaps a testimonial, which will mean peace of mind for you. Or you could use your contacts through LinkedIn, see if they're connected to any VAs, and then ask them if they've used the VA in question or know what it's like to work with them; again, recommendations are always best.

If you don't have a network or don't want to ask people you know directly, you could ask your local community (e.g. Nextdoor), or put a message on a Facebook or Instagram group you happen to be a member of.

Is there a cost?

Yes. VAs cost from £25 an hour upwards, and some work in blocks of time (for example, you can buy a block of, say, 10 hours up front).

1-2-1 assistance

I know only too well how hard it can be to *begin* and take that *decision* to motivate yourself to make changes in your life. This book can be your guide, but if you need that push, a special personal touch and 1-2-1 assistance, then I'd love to be your support, encourager and cheerleader to help you change your life and keep you motivated. For a special offer for my readers, please see the *What's Next?* section (page 195).

Conclusion

We've now come to the end of *Chapter 5*. All of these different forms of assistance will move you forwards on your journey, but I must stress that, at the end of the day, your success comes down to the actions you take and how determined you are to achieve your aspirations, dreams and goals for the future.

Key points:

»   We're 65% more likely to achieve our goals if we're held accountable by somebody, whether it's an accountability buddy, mentor, coach or group. This increases to 95% when we schedule regular accountability sessions to achieve certain goals by a specific time.[117]

»   A coach helps a person to change in the way they wish and aids them to go in the direction they want to go. Primarily, a coach will assist the coachee to develop in a particular part of their life, in their career or to resolve an issue they are facing.[118]

» A mentor can help a mentee set up an action plan to achieve specific career goals as well as provide guidance in other areas of their life.

» Having an accountability partner or buddy helps us to manage our current challenges, provides feedback, acts as a sounding board, shares in our wins and sets goals together with us.

» Being part of a network has become an even more important part of our lives. The easiest way to expand and strengthen our networks is to build on the relationships we have with people we already know: family, friends, colleagues and acquaintances.

» Networking can help with building confidence, and it's a great opportunity to exchange best-practice knowledge, to learn about our peers' different businesses and techniques, and to keep up with the latest developments in our industry.

» A VA is a PA who works remotely and can take off our hands those tasks that may not be within our skill set: social media management, marketing, diary management, event management, bookkeeping and the like.

CHAPTER SIX

MIGHTY MOTIVATION MAGIC MOOD BOOSTERS

In this chapter, I've included some other life hacks I've used that can boost mood, reduce stress and anxiety, and make for a much happier day. Again, remember that if you combine some of these practices and create a hormone cocktail, the benefits are plentiful!

Also, don't forget how powerful time out to have a relaxing bath can be, as is having your hair cut/coloured, your nails done, your eyebrows tidied, your eyelashes dyed, or creating a pamper routine (perhaps once a week or once a month) with a face pack, having a massage or a facial (see page 211 in *Further Resources* for the people I recommend). All of these things will contribute to feelings of well-being, so they aren't to be missed!

Acupuncture

In the past, I've used acupuncture to treat an autoimmune condition (caused by acute stress, so please watch those stress levels!), and I've always come away from a session feeling really good, so I felt I needed to include it in this book, in the hope that it can help others. I have a friend who sees an acupuncturist for migraines, and my brother has always said many positive things about it, as have many other friends of mine.

Acupuncture is an ancient East Asian healing modality that has been in use for more than 2,000 years. Together with herbal medicine, it's regarded as one of the two most pivotal medical skills in East Asian medicines. Fine needles are inserted at certain sites in the body for therapeutic or preventative purposes (and, no, it doesn't hurt; you don't really feel the needles going in unless you have a blockage in a certain area, but then the practitioner will just gently move the needle slightly).

It's used in many National Health Service (NHS) GP practices, as well as in pain clinics and hospices in the UK. It's an effective treatment for anxiety and helps with chronic pain, as it assists the nervous system to achieve balance, stimulates the body's natural feel-good hormones and reduces the level of stress hormones such as cortisol.

Most patients report an improvement in their energy levels, better sleep and a feeling of general well-being.

By calming the body and promoting parasympathetic activity, acupuncture helps to improve circulation and reduce general muscle tension. This enhances all bodily functions that aren't concerned with immediate survival: immunity, digestion, fertility, rest, recovery and repair. Generally speaking, the result is an overall feeling of relaxation and well-being.

My recommendations for practitioners (e.g. Affordable Acupuncture Guildford) can be found in *Further Resources* (see page 211).

Mighty Motivation Magic Hormones: Raises endorphins and reduces cortisol.

Animals

Animals are so good for our souls. According to a study that followed the health records of 3.4 million men and women aged 40 to 80 in Sweden, owning a pet helps you live longer and have a healthier life.[119] They can also rev up your immune system, increase your fitness quota (if you own a dog, or a horse) reduce stress, boost your heart health, enhance social skills in kids with autism, dampen depression and boost your mood.

Research shows that simply petting a dog lowers your amount of cortisol, while the social interaction between people and their dogs actually increases the levels of the feel-good hormone, oxytocin (which is the same hormone that bonds mothers to babies).[120]

I radically changed my work-life balance six years ago, so that I was able to share great times with my little treasure, Billy the Shih Tzu. He brings me and anyone whom he comes into contact with much joy!

An astonishing 84% of PTSD patients paired with a service dog reported a significant reduction in symptoms, and 40% were able to decrease their medications, as revealed in a recent survey.[121] Another study in the US shows that therapy dogs ease the anxiety of cancer sufferers and lift the patient's mood.[122] Furthermore, a 2011 study finds that pet owners have better self-esteem.[123] Another study has determined that pets provide greater social support than humans in mitigating depression.[124]

If you can't have an animal in your home or life for whatever reason, you can always ask to look after your neighbours' or friends' dogs, cats, horses, guinea pigs or chickens; I'm sure they'd be delighted! I've heard that Borrow My Doggie is great, or you could pop down to your local farm, go horse riding at a trekking centre (even better if it's somewhere scenic), walk with llamas or walk with a donkey. Alternatively, you can virtually adopt or sponsor animals through the World Wide Fund for Nature (WWF), Born Free, local city farms and wildlife trusts.

Mighty Motivation Magic Hormones: Raises oxytocin and reduces cortisol.

Birdsong

I love playing birdsong at my vision board workshops; it always gets a great reaction. Scientific research has proven that listening to birdsong is good for focusing the mind, reducing stress, increasing attention, restoring alertness and promoting a sense of well-being.[125]

Scientists at the University of Surrey have been studying the restorative benefits of birdsong and testing whether it really does improve our mood.[126] They discovered that, of all the natural sounds, birdsongs and calls were those most often cited as helping people recover from stress, and allowing them to restore and refocus their attention.

If you happen to live in a big city or missed the birdsong today, and you need some focus and a sense of well-being throughout the day, you can listen to a recording on birdsong.fm, Radio 4's 'Tweet of the Day', or there are plenty of apps and recordings online (YouTube) that you could use instead. Happy chirping!

Mighty Motivation Magic Hormones: Reduces the stress hormone, cortisol.

Breathwork

We take more than 17,000 breaths every day. All of our thoughts and feelings interact with our bodies via our breath. Whether we're feeling stressed, sluggish or anxious, our breathing has the power to make us feel better, as well as to centre us. If we're stressed or worried, our breath is usually shallow. The simple act of taking some slow, deep breaths will always be calming, and it gives us a sense of control.

I was introduced to breathwork when I listened to one of Fearne Cotton's podcasts, featuring Rebecca Dennis (see page 212 in *Further Resources* for details), where Fearne experienced breathwork. Thanks to that episode, I decided to give it a go myself, and I had a session locally in Guildford, Surrey, where I live. I had quite an emotional reaction to the session at the time; it released lots of tension and stress, and thankfully, I left the session feeling relaxed and happy.

Apparently, incorporating just 10 minutes of dedicated breathing practice a day can help us to become more mindful of our needs, strengths and limitations.

Oxygen is the natural resource most needed by our bodies' cells. We can go without food for up to 40 days and without water for three days, yet we get into trouble after just a few minutes of not breathing. Breath equals life.

I don't know about you, but I sometimes forget to breathe! We can practise conscious breathing at any time. In fact, give it a go now. Stop reading and take three slow, deep breaths. Inhale for a count of seven, hold for a count of three and exhale for a count of eight. Feel any different?

Conscious connected breathing detoxifies and strengthens our immune system. Around 70% of our bodies' toxins are released via our breath. A healthy breath can improve sleeping patterns, reduce respiratory issues and improve our digestive system. By releasing tension in the diaphragm and our primary breathing muscles, we can enhance our physical performance in practices such as running, yoga or sports.

There are plenty of breathwork / conscious breathing demonstrations on YouTube, just type in "breathwork" or see the details I have included in *Further Resources* (Alan Dolan and Rebecca Dennis, see page 212).

Mighty Motivation Magic Hormones: Raises endorphins and oxytocin, and reduces cortisol.

Cold-water therapy

Wim Hof, also known as The Iceman, is a Dutch extreme athlete who's noted for his ability to withstand freezing temperatures. He attributes these feats to his Wim Hof Method (WHM): a combination of frequent cold exposure, breathing techniques, yoga and meditation. I came across him recently, mainly due to the wild swimming craze and wondered if there was an easier way of getting this beneficial cold-water fix than finding my nearest swimmable river.

The answer is yes, by taking cold showers instead, and thousands of nutty people from all over the world apparently already incorporate cold showers into their daily routines. The main benefits reported by people who take cold showers regularly are as follows:

* Reduced stress levels – Taking cold showers regularly imposes a small amount of stress on your body, which leads to a process called 'hardening'. This means that your nervous system gradually gets used to handling moderate levels of stress. The hardening process helps you to keep a cool head the next time you find yourself in a stressful situation.

* Higher level of alertness – Cold showers wake your body up, inducing a higher state of alertness. The cold also stimulates you to take deeper breaths, decreasing the level of CO_2 throughout your body, helping you to concentrate. Cold showers seemingly keep you focused throughout the day.

* A more robust immune response – Taking a cold shower increases the amount of white blood cells in your body. These blood cells protect your body against diseases. Researchers believe that this process is related to having an increased metabolic rate, which stimulates the immune response.[127]

* Increased willpower – It takes a strong mind to endure the cold for extended periods of time. By incorporating cold showers into your daily routine, you're strengthening your willpower, which benefits many aspects of your daily life.

* Weight loss – Cold showers (and exposure to cold in general), in addition to increasing your metabolic rate directly, stimulate the generation of brown fat. Brown fat is a specific type of fat tissue that generates energy in turn by burning calories. Hence, cold showers are an effective tool for people who are looking to lose a few pounds.

It's definitely worth having a read about the WHM (see page 212 in *Further Resources*), and there's other research that states it can boost your mood, reduce inflammation and help you to sleep better.[128]

So, if you fancy giving a version of it a go in the shower, then you can try this:

» Shower with your normal warm water.

» Slowly make the water cooler.

» First rinse off your right leg with cold water, starting on the outer side of your ankle. That's the spot farthest away from your heart. Work your way up to the top of the leg gradually. Then rinse off your left leg in the same way.

» Now it's time for your arms: start on the back of your right hand, then move the water up to your shoulder. Next, start at your armpit and move the water down the inside of your arm to your palm. Do the same on your left arm.

» Rinse the rest of your body with cold water. Repeat the previous steps with warm water, then rinse your whole body with cold water one more time.

If you have any issues with your heart or have a weaker immune system, then cold showers aren't a great idea as the sudden changes to body temperature and heart rate may overwhelm your body.

If you're interested in wild swimming with a group, check out Chris Reeves, who founded Win the Morning, Win the Day (see page 212 in *Further Resources* for details), a group that organises morning walks on the beach, followed by a swim in the sea (and now in rivers around the country also, for those of you who aren't close to the sea), all the while breaking the stigma surrounding mental health by talking openly about it. I've joined a group that's run by Michelle Tucker for a swim in Laleham, Surrey. It was just brilliant.

Mighty Motivation Magic Hormones: Raises serotonin, endorphins and dopamine, and reduces cortisol.

Creativity

During the various COVID-19 lockdowns, I experimented with art (as did many others!); in my case, painting with watercolours. This was through online art classes run by an amazing woman called Lynette Pitzolu (see page 212 in *Further Resources* for details). I'd highly recommend her classes, both for adults and for children – just look at the rave reviews! I introduced these classes to my friend Carolyn. She has found a hidden talent in herself and has ended up loving drawing and painting, so much so that she has set up a painting and decorating business!

Research states that painting, pottery or piano-playing – well, whatever gets your creative juices flowing – will boost your mood.[129] Almost 50,000 people took part in the BBC Arts Great British Creativity Test in 2019. The findings show that there are not only emotional benefits from taking part in even a single creative session but that being creative can help you avoid stress, free up mind space and improve self-development, which helps build self-esteem. It's all the more interesting that the survey reveals the most benefit comes from taking part in live creative activities involving face-to-face social interaction, such as singing in a choir or taking part in a group painting class. It has been found that virtual creative experiences also have some benefits, but there isn't as much gain. This just goes to show how important human interaction and connection is for our well-being.

Finally, when we're involved in doing something we love, we get a sense of energy and engagement, and we lose our sense of time because we become so engrossed in what we're doing; it seems to bring on the rapid learning of new information and approaches, and it causes a ripple effect of wanting to use our strengths in a positive way more and more. Do you recognise this in yourself?

So, whatever it is you do – and you'll agree that there are so many activities to choose from, including macrame, flower arranging, painting, playing the piano and calligraphy – the benefits are many!

Mighty Motivation Magic Hormones: Raises serotonin and dopamine, and reduces cortisol.

Forest bathing

You'd probably be surprised to know that a relatively new concept (introduced to the UK only a few years ago) has the potential to be made available on prescription by NHS England. It's called forest bathing, and it's patron is the wonderful Dame Judi Dench.

It was devised 40 years ago by the Japanese Ministry of Agriculture, Forestry, and Fisheries, as part of an initiative to tackle stress among men. The activity involves breathing deeply (and being mindful) and absorbing the atmosphere of a forest as a way of yielding calming, rejuvenating and restorative effects. The effects have been so great that forest bathing is prescribed by Japanese doctors.

The name 'forest bathing' is the English translation of the Japanese term *Shinrin-yoku*, which means "spending quality time, under the canopy of trees, in a forest, for health and well-being purposes".[130]

Research shows that trees really do have healing powers.[131] They release antimicrobial essential oils, called phytoncides, that protect trees from germs and have a host of health benefits for people. The oils boost our mood and immune system function; reduce our blood pressure, heart rate, stress, anxiety and confusion; improve our sleep and creativity; and may even help fight cancer and depression.

I've experienced one of The Forest Bathing Institute's (see page 212 in *Further Resources* for details) Forest Bathing+ events. It was fascinating to learn about the amazing science-backed research on spending time under the trees in ancient forests and the effect it can have on our well-being. With the combination of mindfulness exercises under the canopy of ancient trees and a meditation, I felt completely relaxed and even nodded off for a few moments at the end. I felt very zen all evening and very energised the next day. The effects last for a couple of weeks at least.

The Forest Bathing Institute is now liaising with 11 UK-based universities, and it has several studies in the pipeline, with more planned for the future.

Mighty Motivation Magic Hormones: Raises oxytocin and serotonin, and reduces cortisol.

Giving compliments

When most people receive a compliment, it triggers the same reward centres in the brain that light up during sex, maintains Christoph Korn, a postdoctoral fellow with the University of Zurich's computational emotion neuroscience lab.[132] Furthermore, When we're complimented, we want more of this mini-high.

Sho Sugawara, a researcher with the National Institute for Physiological Sciences in Japan explains that compliments might also help us learn.[133] This research also suggests that, after trying out a new skill – such as cooking, running or playing the guitar – receiving praise seems to improve the brain's ability to remember and repeat that skill.

Appreciation is also fundamental in relationships, both those with our partners/spouses, and those with our friends. It's part of what makes us want to cooperate and collaborate with those around us. If you are faced with a challenge, knowing that you're appreciated helps you to want to work through and overcome that challenge.

Scientists have also found that being paid a compliment actually stimulates the same parts of your brain that are activated when you get paid a monetary award.[134]

Paying someone a compliment can also be a good conversation starter or a good way to get over an awkward lull in a conversation, whether it's a conversation with someone you know or someone you've just met.

In this way, it's not just the receiver who walks away better off. Compliments benefit the giver, too. Being in the habit of giving compliments helps us notice and appreciate what's good and what we like in those around us. Being complimentary helps us create an optimistic, happier outlook.

Compliments are so easy to give, so we should all be doing it much, much more!

Mighty Motivation Magic Hormones: Dopamine.

Helping and volunteering

Happiness is found in helping others. In the words of Gandhi: "The best way to find yourself is to lose yourself in the service of others." We give back because it teaches us to find compassion within ourselves and to stay attached to values that are linked to the common good.

Volunteering in all shapes and forms strengthens our communities, brings people together, and provides us with valuable experience and insight. And when we give time and energy to others, we feel better about ourselves and our communities.

In a study published in 2020 in the *Journal of Happiness Studies*, researchers examined data from nearly 70,000 research participants in the UK, who received surveys about their volunteering habits and their mental health, including their level of well-being and functioning in everyday life, every two years from 1996 to 2014.[135] Compared to people who didn't volunteer, people who had volunteered in the past year were more satisfied with their lives and rated their overall health as better. Additionally, the researchers posit that people who volunteer more frequently experience greater benefits: those who volunteered at least once a month reported better mental health than participants who volunteered infrequently or not at all.

Research suggests that people who start out with lower levels of well-being may get an even bigger boost from volunteering.[136]

Get in touch with your local council to find out about volunteering locally, or google the name of the town or village you live in plus "volunteering", and see what comes up. Alternatively, check if any of your neighbours need any help with anything or put a post on Nextdoor to offer your services.

Mighty Motivation Magic Hormones: Raises oxytocin, dopamine and serotonin, and reduces cortisol.

Kindness / paying it forwards

It's not difficult to be kind, but our busy lives take over. If we just stopped still for a moment and made a pact to be kind or make a kind gesture in the next moment, there would be so many benefits put out into the world.

Even more wonderful are the scientific benefits of being kind. Witnessing acts of kindness produces oxytocin, occasionally referred to as the 'love hormone', which aids in lowering our blood pressure and improving our overall heart health. It also energises us, makes us happy, increases our lifespan, gives so much pleasure (yes, it does!), reduces pain and stress, and much more. Kindness can also be taught; people can actually build up their compassion muscle.

Being kind improves your mood, and one good deed in a crowded area can create a ripple effect and improve the day of lots of people. Research shows that being kind is proven to make people feel more energetic, calmer and less depressed.[137]

Kindness also stimulates the production of serotonin, the feel-good chemical that makes you happy.

Here are a few ways in which we can be kind (and it doesn't have to cost the earth):

* Smile at somebody, say hello and give them a compliment.

* Send somebody a card with some nice words on/in it.

* Help somebody in a practical way without being asked.

* Minimise your judgement and be compassionate instead.

* Be present – put your mobile phone away!

* Look after yourself.

* Share the kindness you receive.

* Buy somebody a coffee/tea.

Mighty Motivation Magic Hormones: Raises serotonin, endorphins and dopamine, and kind people have less cortisol.

Reflexology

Reflexology is a complementary therapy that applies gentle pressure to the feet or hands to stimulate energy pathways in the body, so as to bring about a state of relaxation and to help the body's own healing process.

Reflexology works in a similar way to acupressure and acupuncture. It's thought that there are certain points on the feet and hands that correspond to the organs and glands in the body. So, by pressing and massaging these points, it can stimulate energy pathways in the body. If any energy pathways are blocked, reflexology aims to unblock them, allowing the energy to flow freely again, which seeks to restore balance to the body.

If your reflexologist experiences tender, sensitive or crunchy sensations when massaging your feet, they say it can indicate that an area of your body is out of balance. By pressing the points and working them gently, reflexologists believe that it'll kick-start your body's natural healing powers.

The average pair of feet will walk about 40,000 miles in a lifetime, usually without the Ministry of Transport (MOT) test that we insist our cars have! Just think of a reflexology session as an MOT for the whole body through the feet. A regular maintenance treatment may help to keep the body on an even keel, through its relaxing and calming effects, and may therefore prevent many of the everyday health niggles that we seem to put up with today.

Reflexology can be extremely effective in minimising the effects of stress on the mind and body, for lifting your mood, and for improving your general well-being.

My dad used to see a reflexologist regularly, which he loved, and I highly recommend Lou Matchu (see page 212 in *Further Resources* for details).

Mighty Motivation Magic Hormones: Raises endorphins, dopamine and serotonin, and reduces cortisol.

Reiki

Reiki is a Japanese healing art that was developed by Mikao Usui in Japan in the early 20th century. It's pronounced 'ray-key'. You might also hear it called reiki energy, the Usui system of reiki or therapeutic touch.

The Japanese word '*reiki*' means universal energy. Eastern medicine systems work with this energy, which they believe flows through all living things and is vital to well-being. The energy is known as '*ki*' in Japan, '*chi*' in China and '*prana*' in India. Reiki isn't part of any type of religion or belief system.

A reiki practitioner aims to change and balance the energy fields in and around your body, to help on a physical, psychological, emotional and spiritual level. The practitioner will move their hands around your body. They may touch you lightly or have their hands just above your body. You may experience sensations in the body such as heat or tingling. Some people report seeing visualisations such as colours or pictures, or having memories appear.

I've experienced the benefits of reiki a number of times. I can highly recommend Georgie Pincus, who is based in Ascot, Surrey (see page 212 in *Further Resources* for details). A session of reiki can help you to feel deeply relaxed, can relieve emotional stress and tension, and can also help to improve your overall well-being.

Mighty Motivation Magic Hormones: Serotonin, dopamine, oxytocin and endorphins.

Smiling and laughter yoga

Smiling can lift a bad mood. Even if you don't feel like smiling today or maybe there's no reason to smile, scientists have found that smiling on purpose can help people feel better. Just the simple act of putting a smile on your face can cause you to feel actual happiness, joy or amusement. Smiling on purpose changes your brain chemistry.

There's a saying that laughter is the best medicine, and it turns out that there's some scientific truth to this assertion. The health benefits of laughing include lower blood pressure, a feeling of well-being, a decrease in stress hormones, an increase in the amount of immune cells and infection-fighting antibodies, and improved resistance to disease.

A study of laughter had such successful results that the Laughter Yoga School was formed in a park in Mumbai in 1995, and since then, thousands of laughter clubs and laughter yoga groups have been formed all around the world, showing there's a need to laugh more! When you force a smile, it releases dopamine, endorphins and serotonin into your bloodstream, not only making your body relax but also working to lower your heart rate and blood pressure. Interestingly, primates and apes also enjoy a good chuckle.

If you fancy smiling, laughing or want to boost your mood, try some of the following:

* Watch funny YouTube videos.

* Find a funny podcast.

* Watch a silly/funny sitcom.

* Start a gratitude journal.

* Think of all the funny or happy things that have happened in your life and write them down.

* Create a Pinterest board of lots of stuff that makes you happy.

* Spend time with children.

* Spend time with animals.

* People watch.

* Read a funny book.

* Go to a comedy show.

* Do something silly.

* Listen to music and dance.

* Have a cold shower.

During the various COVID-19 lockdowns, I attended a number of laughter yoga sessions, which I loved; these were run by the lovely Emma Jennings, an old school friend of mine (see page 212 in *Further Resources* for details). The sessions are brilliant!

Mighty Motivation Magic Hormones: Raises serotonin, dopamine and endorphins, and reduces cortisol.

"Happiness is when what you think, what you say, and what you do are in harmony."

– Mahatma Gandhi

CONCLUSION

So here we are at the end of this book. Congratulations for getting to the end; well, nearly the end! I've absolutely loved writing this book, and I'm sad it's finished, but it feels great getting everything in my head from over 4 years of research down on paper, at last!

My hope and greatest wish is that this book proves to be the one you carry in your handbag, pocket or backpack, or leave by the loo, and that you refer to it often, or buy it for a friend or family member as a gift.

I know I've included a lot of facts and information in this book, and there's loads to digest, but hopefully, there are a few modalities, tools, strategies, methods and therapies that you may not have heard about and are open-minded enough to try out. Or perhaps you've been reminded of something you've tried before, liked and forgotten about. And don't forget to keep drinking that water and feeding yourself nutritious food – you'll be feeding your brain at the same time!

What's more, there are plenty of free resources at our finger tips in the form of videos, courses and podcasts, so we really are spoilt for choice.

There are three key points I'd like to make to conclude this book:

1. Self-care is not selfish

There's a reason that self-care is Step 1 in this book: in no way is self-care an indulgence; rather, it's an essential component for preventing stress, overwhelm, anxiety and burnout. Self-care shouldn't be considered as something extra or something that's nice to do if you have the time.

Nor should it be viewed as something you only do if you have time or as a reward that can be gained once other tasks are completed. It needs to be an integral part of our daily lives. Period. Strengthening our emotional, physical and spiritual health through self-care is the foundation and pillar for our overall health and well-being.

Take heed and take care. Please.

2. Create a vision for your future (and find your purpose, if you haven't found it already)

We all need to know where we're going in life. There's a great quote by David Bach: "If you don't know where you're going, you might not like where you end up." And it's true. It leaves you feeling uneasy, drifting and lost at sea, and there's nothing worse than that – you know I know that!

Follow my instructions in the 'Vision board' section in *Chapter 3* (see page 121), or if you get stuck, get in touch with me and let me help you get unstuck, create clarity and discover where you're heading over the next year and beyond.

Lastly, work on finding your life's purpose if you haven't already, as it'll create a sense of meaning in your life and a sense of place; you'll get more of a sense of who you are. It allows you to have a much more profound impact on the world and more confidence, and we all need that from you.

3. Where's my routine taking me?

We all have 24 hours in a day, but how are you spending them? Are they taking you to where you want to be? Or are you leaving things to chance? Is how much you're scrolling through social media on your mobile phone getting out of control?

Because if you aren't moving towards where you want to be, then how do you think you're going to get there? You need to visualise your future and then act on that future in the present, or you won't get there. If you're struggling to get to where you want to be, write down (in your notebook) what's keeping you from where you want to go. Then read through it and cross out the excuses and limitations – most of it'll be fear! Invest in yourself, invest in your dreams, believe you can and you're halfway there. And don't forget to get some help if you're too scared!

It's your time to dream...

"Hope lies in dreams, in imagination, and in the courage of those who dare to make dreams into reality."

—Jonas Salk

WHAT'S NEXT?

As I mentioned earlier, I'm well aware of the difficulty of just getting started when it comes to making a change in your life. Although there's a lot of helpful information for you throughout this book, if you find that you could really use some assistance on a 1-2-1 basis and some more personal encouragement, I'd really love to provide that individual support to facilitate you making a change in your life and keeping you motivated. It's your time to dream big.

With my help you can go from:

- ✓ confusion to clarity;
- ✓ uncertainty to certainty;
- ✓ disconnection to connection; and
- ✓ purposeless to purpose.

As a result, you'll do the following:

- ✓ Discover your true self.
- ✓ Align your goals and actions with your true purpose, and create a life that gives you the happiness and fulfilment you really want.

✓ Cultivate unshakeable confidence in yourself, and learn how to recognise and overcome the limiting beliefs that have been holding you back from achieving your true potential.

✓ Move beyond your comfort zone and ask for what you want.

✓ Take consistent daily actions that result in amazing opportunities, possibilities and achievements.

✓ Persevere in the face of obstacles, until your goals are achieved.

✓ Feel positive and excited about life again.

 You can find my different coaching packages on my website (**www.themotivationclinic.co.uk**), and if you get in touch with me via email at lara@themotivationclinic.co.uk, quoting "The Time Is Now" in the subject line, I'll contact you to schedule a Motivation Magic discovery call.

In addition, for anyone who's kind enough to take the time to leave a review for this book on Amazon, I'd like to thank you with a complimentary place on my Motivation Magic Roundtable, held on the last Friday of every month from 12pm–1pm UK time, where like-minded individuals can gather as a community to share ideas, motivation and inspiration.

I very much look forward to talking with you.

REFERENCES

1. Thomas, B., Fernandoa, S., Klockeb, S., Griepenstroha, J., Aschenbrennerc, S., & Driessenab, M. (2012). Increased suppression of negative and positive emotions in major depression. *Journal of Affective Disorders, 141*(2–3):474–479. https://doi.org/10.1016/j.jad.2012.03.019

2. Holahan, C.J., Moos, R.H., Holahan, C.K., Brennan P.L., & Schutte, K.K. (2005). Stress generation, avoidance coping, and depressive symptoms: A 10-Year Model. *Journal of Consulting and Clinical Psychology, 73*(4):658–666. https://doi.org/10.1037/0022-006X.73.4.658

3. Bastian, B., Kuppens, P., Hornsey, M. J., Park, J., Koval, P., & Uchida, Y. (2012). Feeling bad about being sad: The role of social expectancies in amplifying negative mood. *Emotion, 12*(1):69–80. https://doi.org/10.1037/a0024755

4. Self-care (n.d.). In *Lexico*. Retrieved from: https://www.lexico.com/definition/self-care?locale=en

5. Elrod, H. (2017). *The miracle morning*. London, UK: John Murray Learning.

6. The British Dental Association. (2020). *Fluid (water and drinks): Food Fact Sheet*. Retrieved from: https://www.bda.org/news-centre/blog/Pages/Are-new-diet-fads-wrecking-teeth.aspx?utm_source=facebookwww.bda.org.

7. The Association of UK Dieticians (2020). *Fluid (water and drinks): Food fact sheet*. Retrieved from: https://www.bda.uk.com/resource/fluid-water-drinks.html

8. Wittbrodt, M.T. & Millard-Stafford, M. (2018). Dehydration impairs cognitive performance: A meta-analysis. *Medicine & Science in Sports & Exercise, 50*(11):2360–2368. doi: 10.1249/MSS.0000000000001682

9. Mindfulness. (n.d.). In *Cambridge Dictionary*. Retrieved from: https://dictionary.cambridge.org/dictionary/english/mindfulness

10. Meditation. (n.d.). In *Cambridge Dictionary*. Retrieved from: https://dictionary.cambridge.org/dictionary/english/meditation

11. Simone, F. (2017). Negative self-talk: Don't let it overwhelm you. *Psychology Today*. Retrieved from: https://www.psychologytoday.com/us/blog/family-affair/201712/negative-self-talk-dont-let-it-overwhelm-you

12. Headspace. (2020). *Headspace* (version 3.178.0) [mobile app]. https://www.headspace.com/

13. Goyal, M., Singh, S., & Sibinga, E.M.S. (2014). Meditation programs for psychological stress and well-being. *JAMA Internal Medicine, 174*(3):357–368. doi:10.1001/jamainternmed.2013.13018

14. Walton, A.G. (2015). 7 ways meditation can actually change the brain. *Forbes.* Retrieved from: https://www.forbes.com/sites/alicegwalton/2015/02/09/7-ways-meditation-can-actually-change-the-brain/?sh=6b3756e61465

15. Affirmation. (n.d.). In *Cambridge Dictionary.* Retrieved from: https://dictionary.cambridge.org/dictionary/english/affirmation

16. Merit Motion Pictures. (2016). *The Nature of Things: My brain made me do it* [television programme]. Toronto, Canada: CBC. https://www.cbc.ca/natureofthings/episodes/my-brain-made-me-do-it

17. The Pacer Blog (n.d.). Walking vs caffeine for energy – get a natural energy boost! [blog post]. Retrieved from: https://blog.mypacer.com/2019/11/25/walking-vs-caffeine-for-energy-get-a-natural-energy-boost/

18. Randolph, D.D & O'Connor, P.J. (2017). Stair walking is more energizing than low dose caffeine in sleep deprived young women. *Physiology & Behavior, 174:* 128–135. https://doi.org/10.1016/j.physbeh.2017.03.013.

19. Gomez-Pinilla, F. & Hillman, C. (2013). The influence of exercise on cognitive abilities. *Comprehensive Physiology, 3*(1):403–428. https://doi.org/10.1002/cphy.c110063

20. Hyde, A.L., Conroy, D.E., Pincus, A.L., & Ram, N. (2011). Unpacking the feel-good effect of free-time physical activity: between- and within-person associations with pleasant-activated feeling states. *Journal of Sport and Exercise Psychology, 33*(6):884–902. https://doi.org/10.1123/jsep.33.6.884

21. Pasricha, N. (2017). *Two minute mornings – A journal to win your day every day.* San Francisco, CA: Chronicle Books LLC

22. Cohen, E.E.A., Ejsmond-Frey, R., Knight, N., & Dunbar, R.I.M. (2010). Rowers' high: behavioural synchrony is correlated with elevated pain thresholds. *Biology Letters, 6*(1):106–108. https://doi.org/10.1098/rsbl.2009.0670

23. Fields, L. (2019). 5 reasons walking is better than coffee for an energy boost [blog post]. Retrieved from: https://blog.myfitnesspal.com/5-reasons-walking-is-better-than-coffee-for-an-energy-boost/

24. Oppezzo, M. & Schwartz, D.L. (2014). Give your ideas some legs: The positive effect of walking on creative thinking. *Journal of Experimental Psychology: Learning, Memory, and Cognition, 40*(4):1142–1152. http://dx.doi.org/10.1037/a0036577

25. Davidson, K. (2021). 14 benefits of strength training. *Healthline.* Retrieved from: https://www.healthline.com/health/fitness/benefits-of-strength-training#benefits

26. Visualise. (n.d.). In *Cambridge Dictionary.* Retrieved from: https://dictionary.cambridge.org/dictionary/english/visualize

27. Elrod, H. (2017). *The miracle morning.* London, UK: John Murray Learning. p. 96.

28. Hamilton, D.R. (2018). *How the mind can heal your body.* London, UK: Hay House.

29. Pikörn, I., (n.d.). How visualization can help ease anxiety [blog post]. Retrieved from: https://insighttimer.com/blog/visualization-for-anxiety/

30. Greenberg, M., (2015). How gratitude leads to a happier life. [blog post]. Retrieved from: https://www.psychologytoday.com/gb/blog/the-mindful-self-express/201511/how-gratitude-leads-happier-life

31. Emmons, R.A. & McCullough, D.M.E. (2003). Counting blessings versus burdens: An experimental investigation of gratitude and subjective well-being in daily life. *Journal of Personality and Social Psychology, 84*(2), 377–389. https://doi.org/10.1037/0022-3514.84.2.377

32. Spenst, D., (2017). *The 6-minute diary.* Berlin, Germany: UrBestSelf.

33. Moeller, P. (2012, October 4). Why learning leads to happiness. *HuffPost.* Retrieved from: https://www.huffpost.com/entry/learning-happiness_n_1415568

34. Kwik, J. (2020). *Limitless.* London, UK: Hay House. p. 239.

35. Elrod, H. (2017). *The miracle morning.* London, UK: John Murray Learning.

36. King, C.M. (2018, February 22). 5 scientific reasons to read everyday [sic]. *Blinkist.* Retrieved from: https://www.blinkist.com/magazine/posts/5-scientific-reasons-read-everyday

37. I'm reading, Mom! (2016). 12 amazing facts you didn't know about reading [blog post]. Retrieved from: https://medium.com/@readtoplay/12-amazing-facts-you-didnt-know-about-reading-85f886176a7b

38. Stanborough, R.J. (2019, October 15). Benefits of reading books: How it can positively affect your life. *Healthline.* https://www.healthline.com/health/benefits-of-reading-books

39. Podcast. (n.d.). In *Cambridge Dictionary.* Retrieved from: https://dictionary.cambridge.org/dictionary/english/podcast

40. Smith, J.A. (2016). The science of the story [blog post]. Retrieved from: https://news.berkeley.edu/berkeley_blog/the-science-of-the-story/

41. Statista (2021). *Podcast reach in the United Kingdom (UK)* 2017–2024. Retrieved from: https://www.statista.com/forecasts/1147560/podcast-reach-uk

42. Nowak, K., Ratajczak-Wrona, W., Górska, M., & Jabłońska, E. (2018). Parabens and their effects on the endocrine system. *Molecular and Cellular Endocrinology, 474*:238–251. https://doi.org/10.1016/j.mce.2018.03.014

43. Chatterjee, R. (2018). *The 4 pillar plan: How to relax, eat, move and sleep your way to a longer, healthier life.* London, UK: Penguin Life.

44. Morton, H. (2021), *Eat well run strong.* Portsmouth, UK: Compass-Publishing UK.

45. U.S. News. (n.d.). *Best diets overall.* U.S. News. Retrieved from: https://health.usnews.com/best-diet/best-diets-overall

46. Chatterjee, R. (2019). *Feel better in 5.* London, UK: Penguin Life. p. 102.

47. Bondonno, N.P., Davey, R.J., Murray, K., Radavelli-Bagatini, S., Bondonno, C.P., Blekkenhorst, L.C., Sim, M., Magliano, D.J., Daly, R.M., Shaw, J.E., Lewis, J.R., & Hodgson,

J.M. (2021). Associations between fruit intake and risk of diabetes in the AusDiab cohort. *The Journal of Clinical Endocrinology & Metabolism, dgab335.* https://doi.org/10.1210/clinem/dgab335

48. Zyler, D. (2011). *Color your style: How to wear your true colors.* New York, NY: Plume.

49. Johnson, S.J. (2020). The psychological properties of colour in fashion [blog post]. Retrieved from: https://thriveglobal.com/stories/the-psychological-properties-of-colour-in-fashion/

50. Empower Yourself With Color Psychology (n.d.). Personality color yellow [blog post]. Retrieved from: https://www.empower-yourself-with-color-psychology.com/personality-color-yellow.html

51. Rikard (2015). The psychology of color: A designer's guide to color association & meaning [blog post]. Retrieved from: https://zevendesign.com/color-association/#yellow

52. Shauss, A.G. (1979). *Tranquilizing effect of color reduces aggressive behavior and potential violence.* Paper presented at the 13th Advanced Seminar on Clinical Ecology, San Diego, California. Retrieved from: http://www.orthomolecular.org/library/jom/1979/pdf/1979-v08n04-p218.pdf

53. Zyler, D. (2011). *Color your style: How to wear your true colors.* New York, NY: Plume.

54. Standish, J. (2011). *How not to wear black: And discover your true colors.* Ropley, UK: O Books. p. 24.

55. Standish, J. (2014, December 7). Colours to boost your mood! Don't be scared to clash — scientists have found brighter clothes make you happier! *Daily Mail.* Retrieved from: https://www.dailymail.co.uk/femail/article-2864623/Colours-boost-mood-Dont-scared-clash-scientists-brighter-clothes-make-happier.html

56. Walton, A.G. (2017). 6 ways social media affects our mental health. *Forbes.* Retrieved from: https://www.forbes.com/sites/alicegwalton/2017/06/30/a-run-down-of-social-medias-effects-on-our-mental-health/?sh=16a70f622e5a

57. Fuller, K. (2019). Social media breaks and why they are necessary [blog post]. Retrieved from: https://www.psychologytoday.com/gb/blog/happiness-is-state-mind/201907/social-media-breaks-and-why-they-are-necessary

58. Chatterjee, R. (2021, July 31). See you in September[@drchatterjee]. [Instagram photo/video]. Retrieved from: https://www.instagram.com/p/CR-2ZRjDp4M/?utm_medium=copy_link

59. Kemp, S. (2020). Digital 2020 reports in partnerships with Hootsuite: 3.8 billion people use social media [blog post]. Retrieved from: https://wearesocial.com/blog/2020/01/digital-2020-3-8-billion-people-use-social-media

60. Roberts, J.A. & David, M. (2015). *Baylor study: Cellphones can damage romantic relationships, lead to depression.* Retrieved from: https://www.baylor.edu/mediacommunications/news.php?action=story&story=161554

61. Matthews, G. (2015). *Study focuses on strategies for achieving goals, resolutions* [press release]. Retrieved from: https://scholar.dominican.edu/cgi/viewcontent.

cgi?article=1265&context=news-releases

62. Kruse, K. (2017). Want to get more done? Try taking more breaks. *Forbes*. Retrieved from: https://www.forbes.com/sites/kevinkruse/2017/02/06/want-to-get-more-done-try-taking-more-breaks/?sh=4dd9fe496db4

63. Cirillo, F. (n.d.). *Pomodoro technique*. Retrieved from: https://francescocirillo.com/pages/pomodoro-technique

64. Chunn, L. (2017, May 10). The psychology of the to-do list – why your brain loves ordered tasks. *The Guardian*. Retrieved from: https://www.theguardian.com/lifeandstyle/2017/may/10/the-psychology-of-the-to-do-list-why-your-brain-loves-ordered-tasks

65. Masicampo, E.J. & Baumeister, R.F. (2011, June 20). Consider it done! Plan making can eliminate the cognitive effects of unfulfilled goals. *Journal of Personality and Social Psychology*. Advance online publication. doi: 10.1037/a0024192

66. Walker, M. (2018). Why we sleep: The new science of sleep and dreams. London, UK: Penguin.

67. Walker, M. (2018). *Why We Sleep: The New Science Of Sleep And Dreams*. London, UK: Penguin. p. 7.

68. Casiraghi, L., Spiousas, I., Dunster, G.P., McGlothlen, K., Fernández-Duque, E., Valeggia, C., & de la Iglesia, H.O. (2021). Moonstruck sleep: Synchronization of human sleep with the moon cycle under field conditions. *Science Advances, 7*(5), eabe0465, doi: 10.1126/sciadv.abe0465

69. Walker, M. (2018). *Why we sleep: The new science of sleep and dreams*. London, UK: Penguin. p. 7.

70. EFT Universe (2010). *The EFT mini-manual* [PDF]. Retrieved from: https://s3.amazonaws.com/eft-books/eft-mini-manual/EFT_Mini-Manual.pdf

71. EFT Universe (2010). *The EFT mini-manual* [PDF]. Retrieved from: https://s3.amazonaws.com/eft-books/eft-mini-manual/EFT_Mini-Manual.pdf

72. EFT Universe (2010). *The EFT mini-manual* [PDF]. Retrieved from: https://s3.amazonaws.com/eft-books/eft-mini-manual/EFT_Mini-Manual.pdf

73. Dincera, B. & Inangilb, D. (2020). The effect of emotional freedom techniques on nurses' stress, anxiety, and burnout levels during the COVID-19 pandemic: A randomized controlled trial. *Explore, 17*(2):109–114. https://doi.org/10.1016/j.explore.2020.11.012

74. Environment. (n.d.). In *Cambridge Dictionary*. Retrieved from: https://dictionary.cambridge.org/dictionary/english/environment

75. Sander, L. (2019). What does clutter do to your brain and body? *NewsGP*. Retrieved from: https://www1.racgp.org.au/newsgp/clinical/what-does-clutter-do-to-your-brain-and-body

76. Sander, L. (2019). What does clutter do to your brain and body? *NewsGP*. Retrieved from: https://www1.racgp.org.au/newsgp/clinical/what-does-clutter-do-to-your-brain-and-body

77. Renner, R., (2020). Why pandemic stress breeds clutter—and how to break the cycle. *National Geographic.* Retrieved from: https://www.nationalgeographic.com/science/article/why-coronavirus-stress-breeds-clutter-how-to-break-cycle

78. Renner, R., (2020). Why pandemic stress breeds clutter—and how to break the cycle. *National Geographic.* Retrieved from: https://www.nationalgeographic.com/science/article/why-coronavirus-stress-breeds-clutter-how-to-break-cycle

79. Hayes, M. (2016). Kitchen mayhem can be diet killer, study says. *Cornell Chronicle.* Retrieved from: https://news.cornell.edu/stories/2016/02/kitchen-mayhem-can-be-diet-killer-study-says

80. Vohs, K.D., Redden, J.P., & Rahine, R. (2013). Physical order produces healthy choices, generosity, and conventionality, whereas disorder produces creativity. *Psychological Science,* 24(9):1615–1622. https://doi.org/10.1177/0956797613480186

81. Raines, A.M., Boffa, J.W., Allan, N.P., Short, N.A., & Schmidt, N.B. (2015). Hoarding and eating pathology: The mediating role of emotion regulation. *Comprehensive Psychiatry,* 57:29–35. https://doi.org/10.1016/j.comppsych.2014.11.005

82. McKay, S. (2013). How your friends reduce your risk of dementia [blog post]. Retrieved from: https://drsarahmckay.com/friendship-socialising-dementia-risk/

83. Mineo L, (2017, April 11). Good genes are nice, but joy is better. *The Harvard Gazette.* Retrieved from: https://news.harvard.edu/gazette/story/2017/04/over-nearly-80-years-harvard-study-has-been-showing-how-to-live-a-healthy-and-happy-life/

84. Gallup (1999). *I have a best friend at work.* Retrieved from: https://www.gallup.com/workplace/237530/item-best-friend-work.aspx

85. Blue Zones (n.d.). *Blue Zones Project.* Retrieved from: https://www.bluezones.com/services/blue-zones-project/

86. Fairchild, C. (2012, October 17). Workplace happiness survey finds friends are more important than salary. *HuffPost.* Retrieved from: https://www.huffingtonpost.co.uk/entry/workplace-happiness-friends-over-salary_n_1971110

87. Largo-Wight, E., Chen, W.W., Dodd, C.B.V., & Weiler, R. (2011). Healthy workplaces: The effects of nature contact at work on employee stress and health. *Public Health Reports,* 126(1_suppl):124–130.https://doi.org/10.1177/00333549111260S116

88. University of Exeter (2014). *Why plants in the office make us more productive.* Retrieved from: https://www.exeter.ac.uk/news/research/title_409094_en.html

89. Hurst, P. & Britton, P. (2019, August 25). Plants and herbs are being prescribed to patients suffering from anxiety, depression and loneliness at a GP surgery. *Manchester Evening News.* Retrieved from: https://www.manchestereveningnews.co.uk/news/greater-manchester-news/plants-herbs-gp-surgery-hulme-16814037

90. Wolverton, B.C. & Nelson, M. (2020). Using plants and soil microbes to purify indoor air: lessons from NASA and Biosphere 2 experiments. *Field Actions Science Reports,* 21(Special Issue):54–59 Retrieved from: https://journals.openedition.org/factsreports/6092

91. Etcoff, N. (2006). *New behavioural research demonstrates flowers in the home make a positive impact on our lives* [paper]. Retrieved from: http://community.passiongrowers.com/wp-content/uploads/2010/08/flowersinthehome1017061.pdf

92. Park, S.-H., & Richard H. Mattson, R.H. (2009). Therapeutic influences of plants in hospital rooms on surgical recovery. *Horticultural Science, 44*(1): 102–105. https://doi.org/10.21273/HORTSCI.44.1.102

93. Jones, L. (2020). *Losing Eden: Why our minds need the wild.* London, UK: Penguin.

94. Heath, O., Jackson, V., & Goode, E. (2018). *Creating positive spaces* [PDF]. p. 20. Retrieved from: https://globalwellnessinstitute.org/wp-content/uploads/2018/12/biophilicdesignguide-en.pdf

95. Van den Berg, M.M.H.E., Maas, J., Muller, R., Braun, A., Kaandorp, W., Van Lien, R., Van Poppel, M.N.M., Van Mechelen, W., & Van den Berg, A.E. (2015). Autonomic nervous system responses to viewing green and built settings: Differentiating between sympathetic and parasympathetic activity. *International Journal of Environmental Research and Public Health, 12*(12): 15860–15874. https://doi.org/10.3390/ijerph121215026

96. Royal Horticultural Society. (n.d.). *Houseplants: to support human health.* Retrieved from: https://www.rhs.org.uk/advice/profile?PID=949

97. Lee, M. S., Lee, J., Park, B. J., & Miyazaki, Y. (2015). Interaction with indoor plants may reduce psychological and physiological stress by suppressing autonomic nervous system activity in young adults: a randomized crossover study. *Journal of Physiological Anthropology, 34*(1), 21. https://doi.org/10.1186/s40101-015-0060-8

98. Park, S.-H., & Mattson, R.H. (2009). Therapeutic influences of plants in hospital rooms on surgical recovery. *Horticultural Science, 44*(1): 102–105. https://doi.org/10.21273/HORTSCI.44.1.102

99. Koulivand, P.H., Ghadiri, M.K., & Gorji. A. (2013). Lavender and the nervous system. *Evidence-Based Complementary Alternative Medicine, 2013.* https://doi.org/10.1155/2013/681304

100. Sánchez-Vidaña, D.I., Pui-Ching Ngai, S., Wanjia, H., Ka-Wing Chow, J., Wui-Man Lau, B., & Wing-Hong Tsang, H. (2017). The effectiveness of aromatherapy for depressive symptoms: A systematic review. *Evidence-Based Complementary Alternative Medicine, 2017.* https://doi.org/10.1155/2017/5869315

101. Lakhan, S.E., Sheafer, H., & Tepper, D. (2016). The effectiveness of aromatherapy in reducing pain: A systematic review and meta-analysis. *Pain Research and Treatment, 2016.* https://doi.org/10.1155/2016/8158693

102. Chappell, M. & Davis, J. (n.d.). *Aromatherapy for arthritis relief.* Arthritis Foundation. Retrieved from: https://www.arthritis.org/health-wellness/treatment/complementary-therapies/natural-therapies/aromatherapy-for-arthritis-relief

103. Kar, A. (2011, January 10). Musical chills: Why they give us thrills. *McGill Newsroom Institutional Communications.* Retrieved from: https://www.mcgill.ca/newsroom/channels/news/musical-chills-why-they-give-us-thrills-170538

104. Bigliassi, M., León-Domínguez, U., Buzzachera, C.; Barreto-Silva, V., & Altimari, L.R. (2015). How does music aid 5km of running? *Journal of Strength and Conditioning Research*, 29(2):305–314. doi: 10.1519/JSC.0000000000000627

105. Bhaskar, S., Hemavathy, D., & Prasad, S. (2016). Prevalence of chronic insomnia in adult patients and its correlation with medical comorbidities. *Journal of Family Medicine and Primary Care*, 5(4):780–784. https://doi.org/10.4103/2249-4863.201153

106. Harmat, L., Takács, J., & Bódizs, R. (2008). Music improves sleep quality in students. *Journal of Advanced Nursing*, 62(3):327–335. https://doi.org/10.1111/j.1365-2648.2008.04602.x

107. Trappe, H.J. (2009). Music and health—what kind of music is helpful for whom? What music is not? *Deutsche Medizinische Wochenschrift (German Medical Weekly)*, 134(51–52):2601–2606. doi: 10.1055/s-0029-1243066

108. Values. (n.d.). In *Cambridge Dictionary*. Retrieved from: https://dictionary.cambridge.org/dictionary/english/value

109. Vision board. (n.d.). In *Dictionary.com*. Retrieved from: https://www.dictionary.com/browse/vision-board

110. Swart, T. (2019). *The source: Open your mind, change your life*. London, UK: Vermilion.

111. Davidson, J.E. & Sternberg, R.J. (2003). *The psychology of problem solving*. Cambridge: Cambridge University Press.

112. Miller, K.E. (2021). Can taking a break lead to "aha!" moments? *Psychology Today*. Retrieved from: https://www.psychologytoday.com/gb/blog/the-refugee-experience/202103/can-taking-break-lead-aha-moments

113. Hanke, S. (2018, August 14). Three steps to overcoming resistance. *Forbes*. Retrieved from: https://www.forbes.com/sites/forbescoachescouncil/2018/08/14/three-steps-to-overcoming-resistance/?sh=793ea6695eae

114. Association for Coaching (n.d.). *Coaching defined*. Retrieved from: https://www.associationforcoaching.com/page/CoachingDefined

115. Life Coach Directory (n.d.). *What is coaching?* Retrieved from: https://www.lifecoach-directory.org.uk/content/what-is-coaching.html#:~:text=Coaching%20is%20a%20process%20where,over%20the%20phone%2C%20or%20online

116. Hanke, S. (2018, August 14). Three steps to overcoming resistance. *Forbes*. Retrieved from: https://www.forbes.com/sites/forbescoachescouncil/2018/08/14/three-steps-to-overcoming-resistance/?sh=793ea6695eae

117. Hanke, S. (2018, August 14). Three steps to overcoming resistance. *Forbes*. Retrieved from: https://www.forbes.com/sites/forbescoachescouncil/2018/08/14/three-steps-to-overcoming-resistance/?sh=793ea6695eae

118. Life Coach Directory (n.d.). *What is coaching?* Retrieved from: https://www.lifecoach-directory.org.uk/content/what-is-coaching.html#:~:text=Coaching%20is%20a%20process%20where,over%20the%20phone%2C%20or%20online

119. Mubanga, M., Byberg, L., Nowak, C., Egenvall, A., Magnusson, P.K., Ingelsson, E., & Fall, T. (2017). Dog ownership and the risk of cardiovascular disease and death – a nationwide cohort study. *Scientific Reports, 7*(1), https://doi.org/10.1038/s41598-017-16118-6

120. Petersson, M., Uvnäs-Moberg, K., Nilsson, A., Gustafson, L.L., Hydbring-Sandberg, E., & Handlin, L. (2017). Oxytocin and cortisol levels in dog owners and their dogs are associated with behavioral patterns: An exploratory study. *Frontiers in Psychology, 8*: 1796. https://doi.org/10.3389/fpsyg.2017.01796

121. John Hopkins Medicine (n.d.). *The friend who keeps you young.* Retrieved from: https://www.hopkinsmedicine.org/health/wellness-and-prevention/the-friend-who-keeps-you-young

122. Fleishman, S.B., Homel, P., Chen, M.R., Rosenwald, V., Abolencia, V., Gerber, J., & Nadesan, S. (2013). Beneficial effects of animal-assisted visits on quality of life during multimodal radiation-chemotherapy regimens. *Journal of Community Support Oncology, 13*(1):22–6. Retrieved from: https://pubmed.ncbi.nlm.nih.gov/25839062/

123. American Psychological Association (2011). *The truth about cats and dogs: Pets are good for mental health of "everyday people".* Retrieved from: https://www.apa.org/news/press/releases/2011/07/cats-dogs

124. Brooks ,H.L., Rushton, K., Lovell, K., Bee, P., Walker, L., Grant, L., & Rogers, A. (2018). The power of support from companion animals for people living with mental health problems: A systematic review and narrative synthesis of the evidence. *BMC Psychiatry, 18.* https://doi.org/10.1186/s12888-018-1613-2

125. Winterman, D. (2013, May 8). The surprising uses for birdsong. *BBC News Magazine.* Retrieved from: https://www.bbc.co.uk/news/magazine-22298779

126. Begum, T. (2020). *How listening to bird song can transform our mental health.* Natural History Museum. Retrieved from: https://www.nhm.ac.uk/discover/how-listening-to-bird-song-can-transform-our-mental-health.html

127. Wim Hof Method. (n.d.) *Benefits of cold showers.* Retrieved from: https://www.wimhofmethod.com/benefits-of-cold-showers

128. Inner Fire. (2021). How Wim Hof can help you with depression [blog post]. Retrieved from: https://www.wimhofmethod.com/blog/how-wim-hof-can-help-you-with-depression

129. Fancourt, D., Garnett, C., Spiro, N., West, R., & Müllensiefen, D. (2019, February 5). How do artistic creative activities regulate our emotions? Validation of the Emotion Regulation Strategies for Artistic Creative Activities Scale (ERS-ACA). *PLOS One.* https://doi.org/10.1371/journal.pone.0211362

130. The Forest Bathing Institute (n.d.). *Who are we?* Retrieved from: https://tfb.institute/about/#:~:text=WHAT%20IS%20FOREST%20BATHING,for%20health%20and%20wellbeing%20purposes

131. The Forest Bathing Institute (n.d.). *Science and research.* Retrieved from: https://tfb.institute/scientific-research/

132. Fetters, K.A. (n.d.) Compliments are like mini-orgasms for your brain. *Vice*. Retrieved from: https://www.vice.com/en/article/mg9pex/compliments-are-like-mini-orgasms-for-your-brain

133. National Institute for Physiological Sciences (2012). *A scientific explanation to why people perform better after receiving a compliment* [press release]. Retrieved from: https://www.nips.ac.jp/eng/contents/release/entry/2012/11/post-223.html

134. National Institute for Physiological Sciences (2012). *A scientific explanation to why people perform better after receiving a compliment* [press release]. Retrieved from: https://www.nips.ac.jp/eng/contents/release/entry/2012/11/post-223.html

135. Lawton, R.N., Gramatki, I., Watt, W., & Fujiwara, D. (2021). Does volunteering make us happier, or are happier people more likely to volunteer? Addressing the problem of reverse causality when estimating the wellbeing impacts of volunteering. *Journal of Happiness Studies,* 22:599–624 https://doi.org/10.1007/s10902-020-00242-8

136. Lawton, R.N., Gramatki, I., Watt, W., & Fujiwara, D. (2021). Does volunteering make us happier, or are happier people more likely to volunteer? Addressing the problem of reverse causality when estimating the wellbeing impacts of volunteering. *Journal of Happiness Studies,* 22:599–624 https://doi.org/10.1007/s10902-020-00242-8

137. Braiden, L. (2019). The power of kindness [blog post]. Retrieved from: https://www.behavioralessentials.com/the-power-of-kindness/

138. WebMD (2021). *What to know about oxytocin hormone.* Retrieved from: https://www.webmd.com/sex-relationships/what-to-know-about-oxytocin

139. Bouchez, C. (2011). *Serotonin: 9 questions and answers.* WebMD. Retrieved from: https://www.webmd.com/depression/features/serotonin

140. Bouchez, C. (2011). *Serotonin: 9 questions and answers.* WebMD. Retrieved from: https://www.webmd.com/depression/features/serotonin

141. Bouchez, C. (2011). *Serotonin: 9 questions and answers.* WebMD. Retrieved from: https://www.webmd.com/depression/features/serotonin

142. Cristol, H. (2021). *What is dopamine?* WebMD. Retrieved from: https://www.webmd.com/mental-health/what-is-dopamine

143. Cristol, H. (2021). *What is dopamine?* WebMD. Retrieved from: https://www.webmd.com/mental-health/what-is-dopamine

144. Cadman, B. (2018). Dopamine deficiency: What you need to know. *Medical News Today.* Retrieved from: https://www.medicalnewstoday.com/articles/320637

145. Field, T., Hernandez-Reif, M., Diego, M., Schanberg, S., & Kuhn, C. (2005). Cortisol decreases and serotonin and dopamine increase following massage therapy. *International Journal of Neuroscience, 115*(10):1397–413. https://doi.org/10.1080/00207450590956459

146. Dolan, E.W. (2019). Listening to the music you love will make your brain release more dopamine, study finds. *PsyPost*. Retrieved from: https://www.psypost.org/2019/02/listening-to-the-music-you-love-will-make-your-brain-release-more-dopamine-study-finds-53059

147. Berry, J. (2018). Endorphins: Effects and how to increase levels. *Medical News Today*. https://www.medicalnewstoday.com/articles/320839

148. Berry, J. (2018). Endorphins: Effects and how to increase levels. *Medical News Today*. https://www.medicalnewstoday.com/articles/320839

149. Berry, J. (2018). Endorphins: Effects and how to increase levels. *Medical News Today*. https://www.medicalnewstoday.com/articles/320839

150. DiLonardo, M.J. (2020). *What is melatonin?* WebMD. Retrieved from: https://www.webmd.com/sleep-disorders/what-is-melatonin

151. Melatonin. (2019, October 31). In *Encyclopaedia Britannica*. https://www.britannica.com/science/melatonin

152. Johns Hopkins Medicine (n.d.). *Melatonin for sleep: Does it work?* Retrieved from: https://www.hopkinsmedicine.org/health/wellness-and-prevention/melatonin-for-sleep-does-it-work.

153. WebMD (2020). *What is cortisol?* WebMD. Retrieved from: https://www.webmd.com/a-to-z-guides/what-is-cortisol

154. Scott, E. (2021). *What is cortisol?* Very Well Mind. Retrieved from: https://www.verywellmind.com/cortisol-and-stress-how-to-stay-healthy-3145080

Please do email me at lara@themotivationclinic.co.uk if there are any amendments needed; these were all correct at the time of writing. Please excuse any errors!

FURTHER RESOURCES

The following list has been divided into further reading (books), people and organisations, websites, meditation-related resources, TED talks, motivational videos, and apps.

Further reading (books)
Non-fiction

» Bernstein, G. (2019). *Super attractor.* London, UK: Hay House.

» Burchard, B. (2017). *High performance habits.* London, UK: Hay House.

» Byrne, R. (2000). *The secret.* New York, NY: Simon & Schuster Ltd.

» Clear, J. (2018). *Atomic habits* (illustrated ed.). New York, NY: Avery Publishing Group.

» Dispenza, J. (2012). *Breaking the habit of being yourself.* London, UK: Hay House.

» Dweck, C.S. (2017). *Mindset* (6th ed.). Edinburgh, UK: Robinson.

» Ekstedt, N. & Ennart, H. (2018). *Happy food – How eating well can lift your mood and bring you joy.* Bath, UK: Absolute Press.

» Forleo, M. (2019). *Everything is figureoutable.* London, UK: Penguin.

» Garcia, H. & Miralles, F. (2017). *Ikigai, the Japanese secret to a long and happy life.* London, UK: Hutchinson.

» Gunter, J. (2011). *The menopause manifesto. Own your health with facts and feminism.* London, UK: Piatkus.

» Herold, C. (2018). *Vivid vision.* Austin, TX: Lioncrest Publishing.

» Hill, N. (2016). *Think and grow rich* (classic ed.). New York, NY: TarcherPerigee.

» Kane, C. (2016). *The complete guide to vision boards* [e-book]. Retrieved from: https://www.amazon.co.uk/Complete-Guide-Vision-Boards-Ultimate-ebook/dp/B01N5JAH0M

» Knight, L. (2019). *X Change.* London, UK: mPowr Ltd.

» Kondo, M. (2014). *The life-changing magic of tidying: A simple, effective way to banish clutter forever*. London, UK: Ebury Digital.

» Kondo, M. & Sorenshein, S. (2020). *Joy at work: The life-changing magic of organising your working life* (Main Market ed.). London, UK: Bluebird.

» Kwik, J. (2020). *Limitless. London*, UK: Hay House.

» Lakhiani, V. (2020). *The Buddha and the badass*. Emmaus, PA: Rodale Books.

» Lott, J. & Fox, R. (2021). *Your dream job toolkit*. s.l.: Joanna Lott Publishing.

» Nightingale, E. (2013). *The strangest secret*. s.l.: Merchant Books.

» Pettigrew, M. (2017). *The most powerful goal achievement system in the world*; Scotts Valley, CA: CreateSpace Independent Publishing Platform.

» Tracy, B. (2013). *Eat that frog: Get more of the important things done today*. London, UK: Hodder Paperbacks.

Fiction

» Irving, J. (1990). *A prayer for Owen Meany*. London, UK: Black Swan.

» Roberts, G.D. (2005). *Shantaram*. London, UK: Abacus.

» Suskind, P. (2020). *Perfume*. London, UK: Penguin Classics.

People and organisations

Introduction

» Alva – to help you understand your menopause: www.withalva.com

» Oakley, Kate – Your Future Fit, personal trainer for midlife women: @yourfuturefit on Instagram; kate@yourfuturefit.com

» Newson, Dr Louise R. – GP and menopause specialist: www.menopausedoctor.co.uk

» Proctor, Cathy – hormone replacement therapy (HRT) specialist: @meandmyhrt on Instagram

» Professional organisations:

  • Cruse Bereavement Support: https://www.cruse.org.uk/

  • Mind – Mental Health Charity: https://www.mind.org.uk/

  • National Domestic Abuse Helpline: https://www.nationaldahelpline.org.uk/

  • Relate: www.relate.org.uk

  • Samaritans: https://www.samaritans.org/

  • The Mental Health Foundation: https://www.mentalhealth.org.uk/

  • Women's Aid: https://www.womensaid.org.uk/

  • Young Minds: https://www.youngminds.org.uk/

Chapter 1

- » Anderson, Anna – integrative health coach: www.annaandersoninc.com
- » Harper-Deacon – Jennifer, ketogenic naturopath: www.jenniferharper-deacon.com
- » Kehinde, Aga – well-being coach and EFT practitioner: www.agakehinde.com
- » Linford, Libby – nutritional therapy and functional medicine for autoimmunity and chronic illness: https://libbylinford.com
- » Shoe, Emma – personal stylist and sustainability champion: www.stylingyouwell.com
- » Smith, Carrie – nutritionist and mindful-eating practitioner: www.carriesmithnutrition.com
- » Varghese, Motty – sleep specialist: www.stjamesprivateclinic.ie/mr-motty-varghese
- » Thordsen, Anneke – mind and meditation consultant: www.annekethordsen.com

Chapter 2

- » Brocks, Belle – Annabel Brocks, contemporary British clothing: www.annabelbrocks.com
- » Brocks, Belle – Hawkins Organic, natural grooming products: www.hawkinsorganic.com
- » Declutterers – Julie Philips and Cherry Morgan, https://www.clutterflies.net/; Di Kelly at /www.simplyorganisedhome.co.uk; and Amy Thompson at www.chirp-home.co.uk
- » Hannah Martin Flowers – wedding floristry: www.hannahmartin.net
- » Kate Avery Flowers – luxury floral design, bespoke floristry tuition and wedding floristry: www.kateaveryflowers.co.uk
- » Little, Emily Jane – Faux Bloom Designs, a unique sustainable alternative to fresh floristry for weddings, corporate events, store windows and interior styling projects: www.fauxbloomdesigns.com
- » Lovejoy, Dawn – product consultant on essential oils, dōTERRA, http://www.mydoterra.com/dawnslovejoy

Chapter 3

- » Canfield, Jack – teacher, truth-seeker, storyteller and life changer: www.jackcanfield.com
- » Deschivanovits, Laura – mindset coach: www.linkedin.com/in/laura-de-schivanovits-154aa8b0
- » Ducey, Jake – success coach, inspirational author and college/corporate speaker: www.jakeducey.com

» Eker, T. Harv – author, businessman and motivational speaker: www.harveker.com

» Forleo, Marie – host of MarieTV, entrepreneur and philanthropist: www.marieforleo.com

» Lakhiani, Vishen (founder) – Mindvalley, personal growth learning platform: www.mindvalley.com

» McKay, Dr Sarah – neuroscientist and director of The Neuroscience Academy: www.drsarahmckay.com

» Peer, Marissa – speaker, Rapid Transformational Therapy trainer and bestselling author: www.marissapeer.com

» Robbins, Tony – author, coach, speaker and philanthropist: www.tonyrobbins.com

Chapter 4

» Floyd, Sanae – business breakthrough coach and sales expert (I have worked with Sanae): www.sanaefloyd.com

» Payne, Steve – NLP practitioner and coach, The Academy of Coaching & Training, (www.taoct.uk) and member of www.anlp.org/

Chapter 5

» Anderson, Anna – integrative health coach: www.annaandersoninc.com

» Fricker, Liana – community designer, strategist, facilitator and founder of Inspiration Space: www.theinspirationspace.co

» Hale, Karen – empowerment and public speaking coach: karen@karenhale.com and https://www.linkedin.com/in/karen-hale-8925862b/?originalSubdomain=uk

» Hodge, Emily – leadership and success coach (I have worked with Emily): www.coachingemily.com

» Knight, Lucia – midlife career consultant: www.midlifeunstuck.com

» Lott, Joanna – career coach: www.joannalottcoaching.com

» Vitou, Kat – health, life and wellpreneur coach, and founder of Well+Life+Tribe: www.welllifetribe.com

» Whitten, Alexa – book writing coach (I have worked with Alexa): www.thebookrefinery.com

Chapter 6

» Affordable Acupuncture Guildford (Vahida Diaz and David Gilbert): www.affordableacupunctureguildford.com (or to find a practitioner in your area: www.acupuncturesociety.org.uk)

» Dennis, Rebecca – Breathingtree, breathwork: www.breathingtree.co.uk

» Dolan, Alan – Breath Guru, breathwork: www.breathguru.com
» Jennings, Emma – Brighton Laughter Club and Brighton Cheerful, laughter yoga: www.brightonlaughterclub.org and www.brightoncheerful.co.uk
» Matchu, Lou – massage and facials (and reflexology): www.surreyhillsreflexology.co.uk
» Pincus, Georgie – reiki practitioner and yoga teacher: www.ahappylife.co.uk
» Pitzolu, Lynette – The Art Class, artist and art teacher: www.the-art-class.com
» Reeves, Chris – Win the Morning, Win the Day, physical trainer: https://wtmwtd.org/
» Saunders, Paola – Essential Vitality, employee well-being services (massage) and display screen equipment assessment: www.essentialvitality.co.uk
» The Forest Bathing Institute, forest bathing: tfb.institute/events
» Thorneycroft, Sarah – facials and mobile holistic treatments: www.wildflowerholistictreatments.com

Websites

» The Happiness Planner, list of core values: https://thehappinessplanner.co.uk/pages/list-of-core-values
» Wim Hof Method: https://www.wimhofmethod.com/

Meditation-related resources

Apps

» Calm: https://www.calm.com/
» Headspace: https://www.headspace.com/
» Insight Timer: https://insighttimer.com/

Books

» Alidina, S. & Teach Mindfulness Community (2020). *Mindfulness for challenging times*. s.l.: Teach Mindfulness.
» Chamine, S. (2012). *Positive Intelligence* (illustrated ed.). Austin, TX: Greenleaf Book Group.

Videos

» Lakhiani, V. (2020). *6 phase guided meditation for positive energy* [video file]. YouTube. Retrieved from: https://www.youtube.com/watch?v=p3USG9PEnWY

Other

» Dispenza, J. (2015). *Meditations for breaking the habit of being yourself* (revised ed.) [audio CD]. London, UK: Hay House.

» Gabby Bernstein – meditation newsletter: https://gabbybernstein.com/freemeditations/

» The Honest Guys – meditation resources: https://www.thehonestguys.co.uk/

Recommended TED/TEDx talks

» TED. (2012). *Listening to shame* | Brené Brown [video]. YouTube. Retrieved from: https://www.youtube.com/watch?v=psN1DORYYV0

» TED. (2012). *Your body language may shape who you are* | Amy Cuddy [video]. YouTube. Retrieved from: https://www.youtube.com/watch?v=Ks-_Mh1QhMc

» TED. (2013). *What fear can teach us* | Karen Thompson Walker [video]. YouTube. Retrieved from: https://www.youtube.com/watch?v=OwgWkUIm9Gc

» TEDx. (2015). *Indulge your neurobiology* | Dr Sarah McKay [video]. YouTube. Retrieved from: https://www.youtube.com/watch?v=xiXZVDKRe00&t=700s

» TEDx. (2016). *Isolation is the dream-killer, not your attitude* | Barbara Sher [video]. YouTube. Retrieved from: https://www.youtube.com/watch?v=H2rG4Dg6xyI

» TEDx. (2016). *Make diseases disappear* | Dr Rangan Chatterjee [video]. YouTube. Retrieved from: https://www.youtube.com/watch?v=gaY4m00wXpw

» TED. (2016). *What makes a good life? Lessons from the longest study on happiness* | Robert Waldinger [video]. YouTube. Retrieved from: https://www.youtube.com/watch?v=8KkKuTCFvzI

» TED. (2018). *The brain-changing benefits of exercise* | Wendy Suzuki [video]. YouTube. Retrieved from: https://www.youtube.com/watch?v=BHY0FxzoKZE

» TED. (2021). *How every child can thrive by five* | Molly Wright [video]. YouTube. Retrieved from: https://www.youtube.com/watch?v=aISXCw0Pi94

Motivational videos

» Cranfield, J. (2014). *Motivation for success* [video]. YouTube. Retrieved from: https://www.youtube.com/watch?v=whuNJ6xo064

» Dispenza, J. (2020). *Motivation for every day* [video]. YouTube. Retrieved from: https://www.youtube.com/watch?v=EpOMk1jOzgk

» Ducey, J. (2016). *Knowing this will give you motivation* [video]. YouTube. Retrieved from: https://www.youtube.com/watch?v=ijew8OT1pXI

» Dweck, C. (2014). *Developing a growth mindset* [video]. YouTube. Retrieved from: https://www.youtube.com/watch?v=hiiEeMN7vbQ

» Dyer, W. (2018). *5 lessons to live by* [video]. YouTube. Retrieved from: https://www.youtube.com/watch?v=dOkNkcZ_THA

» Forleo, M. (2018). *How to motivate yourself to start right now* [video]. YouTube. Retrieved from: https://www.youtube.com/watch?v=y1bXe47onAY

» Lakhiani, V. (2018). *These 5 minutes will change you* [video]. YouTube. Retrieved from: https://www.youtube.com/watch?v=G_hNKT6d4Nw

» Nichols, L. (2020). *I can do it* [video]. YouTube. Retrieved from: https://www.youtube.com/watch?v=tj7utbR4rMc

» Robbins, M. (2018). *The secret of self-motivation* [video]. YouTube. Retrieved from: https://www.youtube.com/watch?v=HoWnfCoFdYs

» Vujicic, N. (2021). *Motivation for everyone* [video]. YouTube. Retrieved from: Https://www.youtube.com/watch?v=BRrfGN9R5bw

Other apps

» Nextdoor: www.nextdoor.co.uk

APPENDIX

In this appendix, I'll explain the mighty motivation magic hormones – hopefully, in the simplest of terms.

Oxytocin [138]

Oxytocin, sometimes known as the 'love hormone' is a small but potent hormone (comprised of nine amino acids) and a neurotransmitter secreted by the hypothalamus, which is the part of the brain that has a vital role in controlling many bodily functions.

How's it produced?

It's produced from hugging, kissing, cuddling and sexual intimacy.

What's it responsible for?

It's the hormone that acts as a chemical messenger from the brain, controlling key features of the reproductive system, such as being responsible for contractions during labour, for breast milk letdown (when your body releases milk while breastfeeding), and for sexual arousal and orgasms. It controls aspects of human behaviour and is also responsible for positive emotions, such as trust and happiness. It acts on many organs in the body (including the breasts and uterus).

What does it actually do for us?

It has a calming effect, can influence your emotions and mental health, and may help lower anxiety. One study has found that people who were given oxytocin as a nasal spray before performing public speaking had a lower level of anticipation anxiety. Other studies show that oxytocin helps you to feel trusting and generous.

It also helps in forming social bonds, which gives a burst of feel-good oxytocin. It's believed that when a person suffers from a lack of connection, this is a form of stress that causes their body to release oxytocin and send them looking for interaction with others.

How can we boost our oxytocin levels?

Acupuncture, pets, touch, music, singing, yoga, socialising, gift giving, sharing love and affection, meditation, sex, cooking and eating, and volunteering all boost oxytocin levels.

Serotonin

Serotonin acts as a neurotransmitter, which is "a type of chemical that helps relay signals from one area of the brain to another".[139] Although the brain is where serotonin performs its main functions (and where it's produced), around 90% of our serotonin resides in our digestive tract and blood platelets.

How's it produced?

A unique biochemical conversion process is responsible for producing serotonin: "It begins with tryptophan, a building block to proteins. Cells that make serotonin use tryptophan hydroxylase, a chemical reactor which, when combined with tryptophan, forms 5-hydroxytryptamine, otherwise known as serotonin."[140]

What's it responsible for?

Collette Bouchez describes the responsibility of serotonin as follows:[141]

As a neurotransmitter, serotonin helps to relay messages from one area of the brain to another. Because of the widespread distribution of its cells, it is believed to influence a variety of psychological and other body functions. Of the approximately 40 million brain cells, most are influenced either directly or indirectly by serotonin. This includes brain cells related to mood, sexual desire and function, appetite, sleep, memory and learning, temperature regulation, and some social behavior.

In terms of our body function, serotonin can also affect the functioning of our cardiovascular system, muscles, and various elements in the endocrine system.

What does it actually do for us?

Serotonin can contribute to well-being and happiness.

How can we boost our serotonin levels?

We can gain more through exposure to sunlight, massage, aerobic exercise or yoga, improving our diet, meditation, and remembering happy events.

Dopamine

Dopamine is a hormone and neurotransmitter that's made naturally in the body, but it may also be given as a drug. It's a chemical messenger that helps in the transmission of signals in the brain and other vital areas.

How's it produced?

Dopamine is produced in several areas of the brain, including the substantia nigra and the ventral tegmental area. It's a neurohormone that's released by the hypothalamus. The body makes it, and the nervous system uses it to send messages between nerve cells.

What's it responsible for?

Hope Cristol explains, "Dopamine plays a role in how we feel pleasure. It's a big part of our unique human ability to think and plan. It helps us strive, focus, and find things interesting."[142]

What does it actually do for us?

Dopamine enables neurons in the brain to communicate and control movement. It impacts many aspects of both our behaviour and physical functions such as learning, motivation, sleep, mood and pain processing.[143]

How can we boost our dopamine levels?

To raise your dopamine levels, exercise regularly, meditate, get a massage[144,145] or listen to music.[146]

Endorphins

Endorphins are chemicals that the nervous system produces naturally to help you cope with pain or stress. They can act as a pain reliever or happiness booster, so they are frequently called 'feel-good' chemicals.[147]

How are they produced?

They're mainly produced by the hypothalamus and the pituitary gland, but they can also be made by other parts of the body.[148]

What are they responsible for?

Endorphins reduce pain and boost pleasure, resulting in a feeling of well-being. They're also released during other activities, such as eating, exercise and sex.

How can we boost our endorphin levels?

We can release more endorphins when we take a hot bath; enjoy a massage; get some sun; perform a random act of kindness; make music; watch our favourite film, play or comedy TV show; laugh with friends; eat dark chocolate,[149] have sex; smell aromatherapy oils; meditate; try acupuncture; or do some exercise – any exercise!

Melatonin

Melatonin is a hormone that has long been associated with control of the sleep–wake cycle.[150]

How's it produced?

Melatonin is secreted principally by the pineal gland and mainly at night-time.

What's it responsible for?

Its most important function is in the regulation of sleep cycles (i.e. your circadian rhythm). Its production is guided by the retina in your eye detecting light and dark.[151]

How can we boost our melatonin levels?[152]

To trigger more melatonin production, you should get more sunlight and increase your daylight exposure, particularly in the morning. Try to take time out of your busy schedule to go for a walk. Daytime exercise and natural light exposure will promote regular and higher melatonin secretion at night-time. Develop a regular sleep schedule and get to bed early; late nights can alter melatonin production, making you drowsy during the day but alert in the evening. Melatonin production is increased by darkness, so you may want to consider using blackout curtains or blinds in your bedroom.

Cortisol[153]

Cortisol is nature's built-in alarm system. It's your body's main stress hormone. It works with certain parts of your brain to control your mood, motivation and fear.

How's it produced?

Your adrenal glands, which are triangular organs at the top of your kidneys, make cortisol.

What's it responsible for?

Cortisol plays an important role in various things your body does, including boosting your energy so you can handle stress; restoring balance; controlling your sleep/wake cycle; increasing blood sugar (glucose); regulating blood pressure; keeping inflammation down; and managing how your body uses carbohydrates, fats, and proteins.

How does it work?[154]

The adrenal glands release cortisol in response to stress or fear, as part of the body's fight-or-flight response. When confronted by some type of threat in your environment, your body goes through a series of near-instantaneous reactions that prepare you to either stay and deal with the problem or escape to safety.

The brain structure known as the amygdala alerts the hypothalamus, which then signals a range of responses, including the release of hormones such as adrenaline and cortisol. Cortisol is important for your body to function normally, but too much cortisol can be bad for your health, as it can cause anxiety and depression, headaches, heart disease, memory and concentration problems, issues with digestion, trouble sleeping, and weight gain.

ACKNOWLEDGEMENTS

Who knew that writing a book would turn up on my 2021 vision board, created in March of this year? It was in the form of an image from a magazine that said "Say it. Write it. Share It" no less. I was inspired by Rebecca Newenham, owner of the incredible Get Ahead VA franchise (and a great friend, mentor and encourager), who on her third vision board workshop with me also discovered a book on her vision board, which she then went on to publish (*Virtually Yours*) in November of last year. Thank you, Rebecca, for everything!

A thank you for the encouragement Helen Morton, who published her first book, *Eat Well Run Strong*, last month, showing us all that it's possible to complete a book by dedicating 5 minutes a day to writing. Incredible. Thank you, Helen, for your cheerleading the whole way through my book journey.

Huge thanks and much love go to my wonderful parents, Chris and Karin Doherty, for their never-ending love, support and encouragement over the years. Now you know where I get it from! I very sadly lost my mum, Karin, during the editing process of this book; however, I was so happy to be able to share some of its contents with her before she passed.

Thanks to my amazing girlfriends (in no particular order), whom I couldn't live without and I'm blessed to have in my life: Carolyn, Georgie, Rosie, Bridget, Maro, Georgia, Sarah, Marie,

Jen, Karen, Emma, Belle, Aga, Kirsty, Sue, Tamsin, Lou, Georgie and Anneke. I love you all. Thank you for your support always.

Thanks to my gorgeous aunt Kirsten, who has always been a particularly kind, loving and supportive presence in my life.

Thanks to Rem, for being a brilliant accountability buddy and partner in crime, and for the laughter – does that make sense?

A special thank you to Bex for encouraging me to study for a qualification in coaching, for your amazing friendship and generosity and for falling asleep at all the right moments in my life.

To all of my incredible and extraordinary clients, thank you! Each and every one of you inspires me on a daily basis, and I so look forward to more vision boarding and 1-2-1 work with you. Keep dreaming.

Thanks to Clarence for being the first person I ever coached long term, for introducing me to Dr Rangan Chatterjee, and for encouraging me to carry on coaching and to write more. Mozambique, here I come!

A special thank you goes to my new lockdown friends – Ginny, Chewy and Andrew – for making some of those days all the better for seeing you. Not forgetting being fuelled by the best coffee in Guildford from the amazing team at Krema, and having the pleasure of the beautiful, flower-filled Castle Grounds to walk around.

I'd also like to thank and acknowledge the best boss I ever had – Graham Wainer. Although it's over 20 years since we worked together, I've never forgotten the support and encouragement he gave to me during the 6 years or so we worked together. He also pushed me out of my comfort zone! Thank you, Graham; I have never looked at spreadsheets in the same way since!

Thanks again to all of the inspirational and talented people, coaches and practitioners whom I mention and recommend in this book. I'm continually gobsmacked by the expertise, knowledge and extraordinariness of individuals whom I come across on a regular basis.

Thank you to Alexa Whitten, my book coach (typesetter and publisher), for helping me get this book out of my head on to paper. It has been fun!

To Lindsay Corten, for your exceptional editing skills, thank you so much!

And finally, thank you to Billy for always being that constant, loyal and loving presence, particularly during the late nights finishing this book. I adore you.

Lara xo

ABOUT THE AUTHOR

Lara Doherty founded The Motivation Clinic in 2018. After many years working in the corporate world, she knew there was more to life than meandering through the daily grind, and for the first time in her life, she started to put herself at the top of her to-do list by creating a more intentional, goal-driven and purposeful life, helped by her discovery of the power of vision boards and the wonderful world of neuroscience.

Lara grew up never really being clear on what she wanted to do when she became an adult. Schools didn't know where to place non-conventional, 'creative' types in the 1980s. She fell into various wonderful careers, with strong relationship-building skills, but she was always the super-achiever – working hard and playing hard to the detriment of a conventional life. This, of course, wasn't sustainable and, inevitably, led to burnout.

Funnily enough, a psychometric test many years ago had pinpointed nursing, coaching or journalism as potential career avenues, but it took that burnout and a failed relationship to completely change her life for the better. For the last 3.5 years, as a vision and motivational coach, she has been helping people to get unstuck, gain clarity, and uncover undiscovered potential and opportunities in themselves.

She works with midlife women, helping them to discover their long-forgotten dreams, find their true purpose and determine what they really want to achieve out of life: how they want to present themselves to the world (and to themselves), what they want to do and what they want to have.

Lara loves nothing more than motivating, supporting and encouraging others to fulfil those dreams, just like she's doing right now through this book she has written. It's her biggest wish that this book will be that inspiration, assistance and reassurance her readers need to put themselves at the top of their own to-do lists, and to uncover their unique talents, gifts and aspirations that may be buried inside them, waiting to be revealed.

Now you can dream...

Printed in Great Britain
by Amazon